Embracing Fun in Retirement

Boost Wellness, Build Social Connections, and Explore Affordable Adventures

Danny Toam

ISBN
Hardback: 978-1-965134-98-6
Paperback: 978-1-965134-99-3

Table of Content

CONTENTS

Introduction

Whoever said retirement is a time to slow down clearly hasn't met the vibrant community of today's go-getters aged 55 to 80. If you've recently hung up your hat at work or are about to and find yourself pondering, *What's next?* Let me assure you, the answer is as exhilarating as you're willing to make it. Welcome to your new adventure—retirement reimagined, where every day holds the promise of discovery and joy.

I'm an author deeply rooted in wellness and community service. I've spent years guiding outstanding individuals like you through the transition from a structured work life to a retirement brimming with potential. This book is born out of a passion to see you thrive during these golden years, not just by staying busy but by joyfully engaging in life in meaningful ways.

Embracing Fun in Retirement is crafted to be your companion and guide as you navigate this exciting phase of life. It's packed with practical advice, from how to stay on top of the latest technology to how to find new hobbies that light up your days. We'll explore how to maintain your physical and mental health, delve into the world of affordable travel, and discuss ways to forge new social connections that enrich your days.

I remember a couple, Helen and John, who thought retirement meant endless days of television and quiet living. But through a few simple adjustments and embracing new activities, they found themselves volunteering, traveling to places they'd only dreamed of, and even learning to dance the salsa! Their story is just one of many you'll find in these pages—stories meant to inspire and ignite a spark of adventure in your life.

There's a common misconception that retirement is the sunset of your life's journey. Let's dispel that myth. This book challenges such stereotypes and opens up a world where retirement is just another beginning—a vibrant, active, and fulfilling part of your journey.

From staying fit and embracing technology to discovering new passions and reconnecting with old ones, this book covers a broad spectrum designed to cater to all interests. Whether you're a tech whiz or a gardening enthusiast, there's something here for you.

So, if you are ready to turn the page and start a new chapter filled with health, happiness, and connection, I invite you to join me. Let's redefine retirement together, discovering how these years can be some of the most fulfilling of your life. Let's embrace this journey with open hearts and boundless curiosity. Are you ready? Let's begin!

Chapter 1: Discovering New Horizons

Have you ever found an old jacket you haven't worn in years, slipped it on, and discovered a 20-dollar bill in your pocket? That's retirement. You've just found the time—let's call it the ultimate currency—and now, it's all about how you spend it. Retirement is like entering a grand room full of doors. Each door leads to a different adventure and opportunity. The key? Finding the right doors that open to what truly excites you.

Now, I'm not your typical tour guide with a flag leading you to overly crowded tourist traps. Think of me more as your savvy friend who's been there, done that, and is eager to share the secrets to a fulfilling retirement. Together, we'll discover hobbies and passions that resonate with who you are and who you aspire to become in this vibrant chapter of life. So, tighten your laces or slip on your most comfortable loafers. We're about to explore new horizons that promise to add color, zest, and perhaps a dash of unexpected joy to your days.

Crafting Your Second Act: Finding What Excites You

Identify Personal Interests

Rediscovering what lights your fire isn't merely about filling time; it's about stoking the embers of your passion for blazing a trail for a life that's anything but retired. Start with a simple exercise: Grab a notebook and jot down activities that made you lose track of time before the nine-to-five took over. Was it painting by the lakeside? Maybe solving a challenging crossword over coffee? How about that salsa class you took on a whim during a vacation long ago?

Now, think broader. What's something you always wanted to try but never had the time for? Whether it's brewing craft beer, writing poetry, or even metal detecting, there's no time like the present to explore. And remember, the Internet is a treasure trove of tutorials and communities. Platforms like YouTube can offer beginner guides, while forums on websites like Reddit can connect you with hobbyists who share your newfound interests.

Setting Achievable Goals

Let's turn these sparks of interest into burning ambitions. Goal setting is your roadmap to satisfaction. Begin with small, achievable goals to avoid any feelings of overwhelm. If you're interested in gardening, start with a single potted plant. If drawing has caught your eye, aim to sketch weekly. Celebrate every small accomplishment along the way—each is a stepping stone to more complex goals.

Use the SMART framework to outline your goals: Specific, Measurable, Achievable, Relevant, and Time-bound. For instance, instead of vaguely deciding to play more music, set a goal to learn three new guitar songs in one month. This method not only provides clarity but also a refreshing sense of direction.

Exploring Community Resources

Now, let's swing those community doors wide open. Local community centers, libraries, and even colleges offer many resources that can help you dive deeper into your interests. Many community centers provide classes or workshops that range from tech basics to gourmet cooking. Libraries might host book clubs and writing workshops or even give access to free passes for local museums.

Don't overlook the power of online platforms for community engagement. Meetup.com, for instance, is fabulous for finding local groups that share your interests. Whether you're a budding astronomer or an aspiring chef, there's a group waiting for you. Connecting with these communities deepens your study and connects you to the social fibers that maintain life warm and lively.

Creating a Balanced Lifestyle

Balance is vital in this act of your life. Imagine a stool with three legs—physical, intellectual, and social activities. If one leg is shorter, the stool wobbles. Engaging in a variety of activities enhances your overall well-being and also shields you from burnout.

Physical activities keep your body strong and your mind sharp. Intellectual pursuits, like learning a new language or instrument, keep your neurons firing. Social interactions, from book clubs to dance classes, provide emotional nourishment and a sense of connection. Strive for a mix that keeps you excited about waking up every morning. Remember, a balanced life is fulfilling, and now is the perfect time to sculpt your days into a masterpiece of joyous activity.

As you move forward, keep revisiting and reevaluating your activities. What's thrilling today might be mundane tomorrow, and that's perfectly fine. The beauty of this era is its adaptability. The world is your oyster; retirement is your pearl. Let us make it glow.

Tech for Beginners: Smartphones and Tablets 101

Imagine this: A gadget that fits in your hand but can connect you to the entire world. Yes, that's your smartphone or tablet, and believe it or not, learning to use it is less daunting than you might think. Let's demystify these clever little devices together, shall we? It's like learning to ride a bicycle—initial wobbles included   but soon, you'll be pedaling through digital landscapes with the wind in your hair.

Understanding Basic Functions: Your smartphone is essentially a pocket-sized computer. The primary functions include making calls and sending texts, but there's so much more. Every smartphone or tablet has a *home* button; think of it as your go-back-to-start button whenever things get confusing. To make a call, you simply tap the phone icon, and voila, dial a number or tap a contact. Texting works similarly; tap the messages icon to type words and send pictures or even funny GIFs to your grandkids. Apps are the magic doors to everything from games to weather reports. Downloading them from your device's store is as simple as tapping "Install," and remember, many helpful apps are entirely free!

Now, adjusting settings such as text size or brightness can make your device more straightforward to use. Look for the settings gear icon, tap it, and explore options like "display" for visual adjustments. Playing around with these settings won't break anything, so change them as often as you like until you're comfortable.

Safety and Security Tips: As wonderful as technology is, it has its pitfalls. Scammers often target seniors, but you can stay safe with simple tips. First, always create strong passwords that include a mix of letters, numbers, and symbols; think of a memorable phrase or long word and swap out some letters with numbers and symbols. For example, "GrandmaLovesCookies" can become "Gr@ndm@L0vesC00kies!" Secondly, never share personal information like your social security number or bank details over the phone or online unless you are sure of the person's identity or the website's authenticity.

Be wary of emails or messages that ask you to click on unknown links; these could lead to fraudulent sites that steal your personal information. If an email or online offer seems too good to be true, it probably is. When in doubt, consult a trusted family member or friend before acting.

Connecting With Family and Friends: Keeping in touch with loved ones has never been easier. Social media platforms like Facebook allow you to see photos and updates from family and friends all in one place. You can *like* photos, comment on posts, or share your experiences. Apps like Skype, WhatsApp, and FaceTime also offer video calling, a fantastic way to catch up face-to-face, even if you're continents apart. The key here is downloading the app, creating an account, and adding your family and friends to your contacts. Most apps have a search function where you can type in a name. Simply click "add" to include them in your contacts.

Accessing Entertainment and Information: Your device is a gateway to endless entertainment options and a wealth of information. Want to read the latest bestsellers or classic novels? Download apps like Kindle or Audible for ebooks and audiobooks. Are you curious about world news or want a recipe for tonight's dinner? Use the browser app to search the internet or specific news apps like BBC or CNN. Streaming services like Netflix or Hulu offer movies and TV shows at your fingertips; just create an account, and you're ready to watch. Remember, many libraries offer free access to digital books, magazines, and even movies through their websites, so check with your local library.

Navigating this digital landscape might seem like learning a new language, but once you start speaking it, you'll discover a world of opportunities and conveniences. Remember, every expert was once a beginner, and with some practice, you'll find that these smart devices make life easier and a lot more fun. So, take the plunge, press a few buttons, and see where this adventure takes you.

The Joy of Blogging: Sharing Your Stories Online

Have you ever considered that your life's stories and wisdom could inspire someone else? Or that your hobby, whether knitting cozy sweaters or rebuilding vintage cars, could be a beacon for others sharing your passion? Welcome to the world of blogging, a splendid platform where your voice can echo across continents. It connects you with like-minded souls and curious learners. Starting a blog might sound like venturing into the tech jungle, but I assure you, it's more like a stroll in the park with the right guide.

First, choose a blogging platform—that's your first step. Think of it as picking the neighborhood before you build your house. Platforms like WordPress, Blogger, and Medium offer user-friendly interfaces with plenty of guidance for newcomers. WordPress, for example, powers a good chunk of the internet. It is versatile enough to host everything from a minimalist writer's diary to a multimedia-heavy travel blog. Most platforms are free for their basic packages, which is perfect when dipping your toes in the water. Setting up your blog involves choosing a template; this is the fun part where you can decide how your blog looks. Want something clean and simple? Or perhaps you prefer something a touch more sophisticated with elegant fonts and a splash of color? Click through the options and preview them live on your site. Keep experimenting until you find a design that feels like home.

Now, on to the heart of your blog: the content. This is where your personality shines through. But before you start sharing, here's a snippet of advice: Consistency is vital. Plan to post regularly, be it weekly or bi-monthly, so your readers know when to expect a gem in their inboxes. What to write about? Ah, the possibilities! Share stories from your past, lessons you've learned, or tips on a hobby you've mastered. Remember, your unique perspective is what will draw readers. To keep your content engaging, mix your posts with personal stories, how-to guides, and lists. Add the occasional video if you're feeling adventurous. Photos also add color and life to your narrative. Sprinkle in a few when you can to enhance your posts.

Engaging with your community is the cherry on top. Blogs are about more than just sharing your opinions; they are also about starting conversations and developing relationships. Encourage your readers to leave comments, ask questions, and share their experiences.

Respond to their comments to keep the conversation going and show that you value their input. This engagement will transform your blog from a one-way street into a bustling town square.

Safety, though, should never be an afterthought. As you share your life online, remember to safeguard your privacy. Avoid sharing overly personal information like your home address or financial details. Be cautious about public Wi-Fi when uploading content, and consider investing in a Virtual Private Network (VPN) if you're often blogging on the go. A VPN encrypts your internet connection, keeping your online activities private from prying eyes.

Blogging is more than just a pastime; it's a powerful way to share your journey and insights. It connects you to a global village, enriches your retirement life, and might be fun. Who knows, your blog could inspire, comfort, or even change someone's life halfway around the globe. So, why not give it a shot? Your next chapter could be just a post away.

Photography for Everyone: Capturing Moments

Ah, photography! It's not just about snapping pictures; it's about capturing moments, freezing time in a frame, and often, rediscovering the beauty in the everyday. Whether it's a grandchild's smile, the sun setting over your favorite vacation spot, or simply a new recipe you tried, each photograph tells a story. Each image captures a unique moment and adds depth to your personal narrative. And the best part? You don't need to be a professional to start. With a few tips and the right equipment, you can begin this incredible visual storytelling journey.

Choosing the right camera or smartphone is your first step. Think of it as choosing a new friend to accompany you on your adventures. You want one that understands your needs and fits your lifestyle. If simplicity is your mantra, a point-and-shoot camera might be perfect for you. These are generally compact, easy to use, and can produce some stunning shots without needing to fiddle with complex settings. For those who don't mind a bit more complexity in exchange for control over their images, a digital single-lens reflex (DSLR) or a mirrorless camera might be the way to go. These cameras come with interchangeable lenses and manual settings that can cater to various photographic styles—from portraits to landscapes.

Now, if you're thinking, *But I already have a smartphone in my pocket*, you're in luck! Modern smartphones are equipped with cameras that can rival traditional cameras. They are perfect for photographers who want to capture high-quality photos without carrying extra gear. Plus, smartphones are incredibly user-friendly. Look for phones with features like optical zoom, image stabilization, and manual mode options. These features will give you more control over your photography.

Once you've got your gadget, it's time to master some basic photography skills. Let's talk about framing first. Imagine your camera's viewfinder is split into nine equal sections by two horizontal and two vertical lines. Placing your subject along these lines or at their intersections can help create a more balanced composition pleasing to the eye, a technique known as the rule of thirds. Next, the focus is crucial. Most cameras and smartphones allow you to tap on the screen to sharpen the view. As for lighting, natural light is your best friend. Try to take photos during the golden hours— shortly after sunrise or before sunset—when the light is softer and warmer. If you're indoors, use windows to illuminate your subject.

Photography also serves as a powerful form of expression. It's a tool for storytelling, a way to express your emotions and share your perspective with the world. Why not document your adventures and the scenes of your daily life? Each image you capture is a reflection of how you see the world. As you grow more comfortable with your camera, you'll start to see beauty in the mundane, notice the play of shadows and light, and capture emotions and moments that others might overlook.

Finally, sharing your photographs can be just as rewarding as taking them. In today's digital age, social media platforms like Instagram and Facebook are popular spaces for sharing images. They allow you to keep your family and friends updated on your life's visual journal while also connecting with other photography aficionados. For a more tangible keepsake, consider printing your photos. Online services and local stores offer printing options that turn your digital memories into beautiful prints, albums, or even canvas art. Whether you're tech-savvy or prefer keeping it simple, sharing your work can help foster connections and bring joy to you and those around you.

So, grab your camera or phone and start capturing the beauty around you. Every photograph you take is a step further in exploring this artful hobby, and each click adds depth to your days and stories to your life's collection.

Rediscovering Music: Learning an Instrument After 60

The sweet sound of music! It's not just background noise; it's a powerful force that can enhance your life in many ways, especially as you step into the freedom-filled days of retirement. Think about it; music has been a companion throughout your life, from those rock 'n' roll teen years to the lullabies you might have hummed to your children. Now, it's your turn to pick up an instrument and perhaps create some tunes. Whether you're jazzed about jazz, have a penchant for classical, or want to strum along to some blues, learning to play an instrument can be a doorway to enhanced cognitive function. It also improves hand-eye coordination and provides a world of joyous therapeutic activity. Embracing music offers both mental and emotional benefits.

Why should you consider tickling the ivories or strumming the guitar strings at this stage in life? Studies have shown that learning music can keep your brain engaged and help maintain cognitive health. It's like sending your brain to the gym, where you're navigating scales and chords instead of lifting weights. This mental workout can improve your memory, sharpen your problem-solving skills, and even increase your multitasking ability. And let's talk about hand-eye coordination; managing to hit the correct guitar fret or piano key means your brain and hands work in a beautifully synchronized ballet. Plus, the joy and satisfaction of playing a musical piece can lift your spirits and serve as a fantastic stress reliever. Who doesn't want a dose of feel-good hormones serenading through their body?

Choosing the right instrument is crucial because it needs to resonate with your physical capabilities and musical tastes. If arthritis or joint pain is a concern, a keyboard with light touch sensitivity is ideal, or a ukulele, which is easier on the fingers than a guitar. Consider your living space as well; while a set of drums might stir your soul, your neighbors might not appreciate a budding drummer. Digital music software lets you compose and experiment with music virtually without needing large instruments.

Now, where to find lessons? The world is your oyster here, thanks to the internet. Many websites offer courses tailored for beginners and designed explicitly with senior learners in mind. Websites like MasterClass or YouTube have a plethora of tutorials available at your fingertips. For those who prefer a more personal touch, local music schools often offer classes for adults and don't overlook community colleges, which might provide affordable options, too. These settings not only provide instruction but also the invaluable benefit of social interaction. Consider taking a class and meeting other music aficionados who share your passion for melodies. New connections are ready to be formed!

But why stop at just taking lessons? Participating in community music groups can be the cherry on your musical adventure. Playing with others can be incredibly rewarding, whether it's a choir, a band, or a casual jam session. It's a chance to connect, share, and create music together, enhancing your skills and perhaps even performing at local events or family gatherings. This type of community involvement can enrich your musical journey, providing a sense of belonging and an outlet for artistic expression. So, look around for community bands, choirs, or even music nights at your local cafe. You'll be amazed at how music can bring people together. It creates a symphony of friendships and shared experiences.

In the grand symphony of life, retirement is a splendid time to embrace new pursuits, and music offers a world of rhythms and melodies just waiting to be explored. So go ahead, choose an instrument, and let the music play! It's never too late to start, and the benefits can resonate deeply in your life, bringing harmony to your days and joy to your soul. Whether you're mastering a new chord or performing a solo at a local gathering, the magic of music is a timeless gift that keeps on giving. Keep your tunes flowing and your spirits high, and who knows? This musical chapter might just be your best yet.

Gardening With Ease: Tools and Techniques for the Aging Gardener

Ah, gardening! There's something genuinely timeless about the feel of soil under your fingernails and the joy of watching something you planted grow. But let's face it: As much as our spirits are willing, sometimes our bodies beg to differ, especially regarding the more demanding physical aspects of gardening. You'll be amazed at how music can bring people together. It has the power to create a sense of unity and connection. This often results in a symphony of friendships and shared experiences.

First things first, let's talk about the magic of ergonomic tools. These are not your average garden variety tools; they are specifically designed to reduce strain on your body. Ergonomic tools often feature longer handles, meaning you won't have to bend or stoop as much. Tools with padded and curved handles also ensure better grip and comfort, which is excellent for those with arthritis or limited hand strength. Imagine wielding a lightweight yet sturdy trowel that feels like an extension of your hand. As you dig into the earth to plant some cheerful marigolds, the tool makes the task effortless. Consider using a garden kneeler, which provides cushy support for your knees. It can also be flipped over to serve as a handy seat. These tools aren't just functional; they redefine what it means to garden comfortably.

Now, let's elevate your gardening literally and figuratively with raised garden beds. Raised beds are a game-changer; they bring the garden to you. These beds can be built or bought at various heights so you can garden without ever bending over. Fill them with your favorite plants, from fragrant herbs to robust vegetables, and garden away with ease. There's also the stylish option of vertical gardening. Vertical gardens let you grow plants in stacked tiers or on trellises, saving space and transforming a bland wall into a lush tapestry. Both vertical and raised gardens reduce physical strain and add charm to your yard, making it a focal point.

Gardening is not just about beautifying your yard; it's a profoundly therapeutic activity. The physical benefits are evident, as gardening can help enhance your mobility and flexibility. It's a gentle way to exercise without feeling like you're exercising. Then there's the mental aspect; spending time in nature can significantly reduce stress and enhance mood. The act of cultivating plants, from seeding to pruning, can provide a tremendous sense of fulfillment and success. There's something incredibly grounding about connecting with the earth, a reminder of the cycle of life and growth. Plus, the vitamin D boost from the sunshine is a great bonus for your overall health.

Let's not forget the more profound connection with nature that gardening fosters. In our fast-paced digital world, gardening offers a precious pause, a chance to engage with the natural world at your own pace. It's about watching a bee lazily buzz from flower to flower or noticing the dew on a spider's web in the early morning light. These moments, often overlooked, can bring a profound sense of connection to the world around you. They remind us that we are part of a larger ecosystem, a community of living things that thrive on care, attention, and love.

So, remember that gardening is for everyone, whether you're a seasoned gardener adjusting to how your body now prefers to garden or you're just starting to explore this wonderful hobby. With adaptive tools and techniques, you can continue to engage in this enriching activity and transform it into a form of joyful expression that nurtures both your garden and your well-being. Let the plants you nurture in your garden reflect the care you take of yourself—gently, thoughtfully, and with plenty of room for growth and renewal. Gardening also offers plenty of mental and physical health benefits. Remaining physically active and fit is one of the most important things you can do for yourself after retirement, as you will see in the next chapter.

Chapter 2: Staying Physically Active

The utmost necessity of physical activity after retirement can neither be denied nor ignored. Gone are the days of squeezing gym sessions between work meetings or juggling family commitments. Now, it's all about moving at your pace, finding joy in motion, and embracing activities that keep your body engaged and bring a smile to your face. Imagine replacing the treadmill with a laughter-filled yoga session or serene morning stretches with a garden view. Physical activity doesn't have to be a chore; it can be your new favorite hobby!

One of the most delightful ways to stay active without feeling like you're doing a day's work is chair yoga. Yes, you heard that right—yoga, but make it comfy. Chair yoga is a fantastic way to enjoy yoga's benefits without getting down on a mat. It's perfect if you're dealing with joint sensitivity or if the thought of balancing on one foot brings more anxiety than excitement. Let's dive into how chair yoga can be your gentle companion in maintaining flexibility and strength, all from the comfort of your chair.

Chair Yoga: A Gentle Path to Flexibility and Strength

Understanding Chair Yoga

It sounds precisely like chair yoga—yoga performed with the aid of a chair. This form of yoga adapts traditional yoga poses so that they can be performed while seated, making it an excellent option for those with limited mobility or balance issues. But don't let the chair fool you; it's not just sitting around. Chair yoga offers a workout with spinal twists and leg lifts, enhancing flexibility and muscle strength without stressing your joints.

Imagine doing a cat-cow stretch: Seated comfortably, you arch your back, lifting your chest as you inhale, rounding your spine as you exhale, a perfect stretch for your back and shoulders. Or a seated pigeon pose, where one foot rests on the opposite knee, and you lean forward gently, stretching your hip and letting the stress melt away. These are just glimpses of the myriads of movements you can perform, even while seated.

Basic Poses and Routines

Let's walk through a simple routine to get a feel for chair yoga. Start with a seated mountain pose: Sit upright, feet flat on the floor, hands resting on your knees, and take a few deep breaths. Feel your spine lengthening as if a string were pulling you up from the crown of your head. Next, transition to a seated forward bend. Inhale deeply, and as you exhale, hinge on your hips and fold forward, letting your hands slide down your legs. This move is terrific for stretching your back and shoulders.

For balance and leg strengthening, try the seated eagle pose. Cross one leg over the other and hook your foot behind the opposite calf, if possible. Wrap your arms in the opposite direction, hands coming together in front of your face. Hold, breathe, and feel the stretch in your shoulders and legs. Finish with a seated twist: Turn your upper body to one side, using your chair's backrest as support—a fantastic twist for your spine.

Health Benefits

The benefits of chair yoga extend far beyond flexibility. Its regular practice can significantly enhance joint health, making it easier to perform daily activities. The poses help improve balance, which is crucial in preventing falls—a common concern as we age. Moreover, the gentle movements aid in maintaining muscle tone and improving cardiovascular health, which is essential to overall well-being.

But perhaps one of the most appreciated benefits is the reduction in anxiety and stress. The mindful breathing and meditative aspects of yoga are known for their calming effects on our minds. Regular chair yoga sessions can help you manage stress, promote better sleep, and improve your mood overall. It's not just a workout for the body but a soothing balm for the brain as well.

Incorporating Mindfulness and Breathing

One needs to perfectly combine mindfulness and focused breathing into practice to enhance the mental benefits of chair yoga. Mindfulness involves being fully present in the moment, aware of your breath and how your body feels as you move through each pose. This can heighten yoga's stress-relieving effects, making each session a tranquil retreat from the hustle and bustle of daily life.

A simple breathing technique to include is diaphragmatic breathing or belly breathing. Sit comfortably, place one hand on your belly, and breathe deeply through your nose, feeling your belly rise and fall. This action encourages full oxygen exchange and significantly reduces heart rate and blood pressure, fostering relaxation and focus.

Adding chair yoga into your routine is like giving your body and mind a daily mini-vacation. It's about taking that moment to stretch, breathe, and align your body and spirit. With chair yoga, you can turn any chair into your wellness oasis, proving that staying active and healthy doesn't have to be a strenuous endeavor; it can be as simple as sitting down.

Walking Clubs: Socialize and Stay Fit

Imagine this:

- A sunny morning
- A group of friendly faces
- A trail that stretches invitingly before you

That's the charm of a walking club. It's not just about staying fit; it's about weaving the fabric of friendship while taking in some fresh air. If you're intrigued by the idea of starting a walking club in your local area, you're already on the path to adding a delightful chapter to your retirement days.

Starting a walking club is simpler than you think. The first step is reaching out to potential members. You could start with friends or neighbors, but feel free to widen the circle. Community centers, bulletin boards, and social media platforms are excellent places to drum up interest. A simple post like, "Join me for a morning walk this Saturday at [local park]—let's get moving together!" can attract fellow enthusiasts. When choosing routes, consider accessibility and variety. A mix of scenic parks, easy trails, and engaging urban walks keeps the routine exciting and accommodates members of different fitness levels. Regular schedules, such as Tuesday and Thursday mornings, help members plan their week around these energy-boosting meetups, making it easier to maintain regular attendance.

Safety, of course, should be a priority. Always remind club members to wear appropriate footwear—think sturdy, comfortable walking shoes that cushion and support the feet. Weather-appropriate clothing, like breathable fabrics for summer and layered, warm attire for cooler months, ensures everyone is comfortable regardless of the season. It's also crucial to stay hydrated. Encourage everyone to bring a water bottle, and plan routes where you can refill it if necessary. For those needing them, walking aids like canes or walkers should be encouraged; there's no pride lost in making a walk more enjoyable and safer.

The social benefits of a walking club are a beautiful aspect of this activity. Walking alongside others naturally fosters conversation and camaraderie. It's about sharing stories, exchanging smiles, and supporting each other—physically, emotionally, and mentally. The rhythmic nature of walking allows for conversations ranging from light-hearted banter to deep, meaningful exchanges. For many, these interactions become essential to their social life, enriching their days and leading to friendships extending beyond the walking trails.

To keep the walks exciting and challenging, bring variations. Not all walks need to be leisurely. Some days could be dedicated to speed walking, where the group picks up the pace, gets the heart rate up, and adds a healthy challenge to the routine. On other days, consider themed walks, like a photography walk where members bring cameras and stop to capture moments of beauty, or a nature walk focused on bird watching or identifying plants. For those who enjoy more adventure, occasional hiking trips to nearby trails can provide a remarkable change of scenery and a gratifying challenge. These variations keep the body moving in new ways and keep the mind engaged and enthusiastic about what each walk might bring.

Now, we know that a walking club offers more than physical exercise; it provides a gateway to building a vibrant and supportive community. It's about taking steps together, not just on the path, but towards forging lasting bonds and creating joyful moments. As you lace up your walking shoes and step out to meet your fellow walkers, you're working out your body and enriching your heart and soul with friends who share your journey. So, why wait? The right time to start a walking club is now, and the benefits are endless, just like the paths you'll explore in this journey.

Aquatic Exercises for Joint Health

Whoever said exercise needs to be hard-hitting never got the memo about the buoyant bliss of aquatic exercises. Picture this: you, the water, and a series of movements that feel more like a dance than a workout. Whether you're slicing through the water with each swim stroke or laughing through a spirited session of water aerobics, aquatic exercises are a gentle yet effective way to boost your physical health, especially for those of us wanting to take it easy on the joints.

Water is naturally a resistance medium, which means every movement you make helps build muscle strength and endurance without the harsh impact of traditional land exercises. Imagine trying to run underwater; the water's resistance makes your muscles work harder, yet it feels gentler and more fluid. This resistance, coupled with buoyancy—water's lovely way of making you feel lighter— reduces the strain on joints that might feel stiff or sore on land. This makes aquatic exercises a fantastic option if you're dealing with arthritis or any other joint-related issues. Plus, the hydrostatic pressure that water exerts on your body helps improve your cardiovascular fitness by making your heart work harder to pump blood. It's a whole-body workout disguised as a splashy good time.

Now, what kind of aquatic exercises can you plunge into? For starters, there's water aerobics, which isn't just in a wetter setting. It's a fun, social workout that can be as gentle or vigorous as you like. Picture a group of friends moving to music, perhaps using foam noodles or water weights to challenge the routine. Then, there's lap swimming, a tranquil yet powerful exercise that enhances muscle strength, lung capacity, and stamina. And let's not forget about water walking or jogging—a more straightforward yet effective workout that involves walking or jogging in waist-deep or deeper water. It's like giving your legs a massage while you work out; the water's pressure feels soothing against your muscles and joints.

Finding the right spot for these water-based adventures is critical. Your local YMCA, fitness club, or community center might have a pool offering senior-friendly aquatic classes. These places often provide classes tailored to different fitness levels and abilities, ensuring everyone, from beginners to seasoned swimmers, can find a comfortable pace. Plus, joining a class is a fantastic way to meet other aquatic enthusiasts who share your zeal for staying active in a fun, supportive environment. If you need help figuring out where to start, a quick call to local fitness centers or browsing their online schedules can lead you to the right pool. Remember to check if they offer trial classes. What better way is there to dip your toes in the water?

Before you dive in, let's talk gear and safety—because even the calm waters of a pool require some prep. First up, invest in a good pair of water shoes. These aren't just shoes; they're designed to provide traction on slippery pool floors, keeping you stable and safe as you move. They also protect your feet from rough surfaces and keep you comfortable throughout your workout. A flotation device might also be a good idea, especially if you're not confident in your swimming skills. These can help you stay afloat, allowing you to focus on your exercises without worry. And, of course, safety is paramount. Always check with your doctor before starting any new exercise regimen, especially if you have health concerns. Once cleared, warm up before diving into more challenging exercises, and stay hydrated—yes, even in the water. It's easy to overlook, but your body loses fluids as you exercise, even when surrounded by water.

Aquatic exercises offer a refreshing twist to staying fit. They combine the therapeutic effects of water with the joy of movement, making them a perfect choice for those looking to stay active without putting too much strain on their bodies. Whether you're gliding through the water or laughing through an aerobics routine, these water workouts will lift your spirits and your heart rate, all in the embrace of soothing waters. So, why wait? The pool beckons; it's about time you answered the call. Dive into the world of aquatic exercises, and let the water be your guide to a fitter, happier you.

Tai Chi: Meditation in Motion for Balance and Peace

Have you ever watched someone practice Tai Chi? It's almost like observing a slow-motion dance, with each movement flowing smoothly into the next. This ancient Chinese martial art, often described as meditation in motion, is not just about physical movement; it's about developing balance, calmness, and harmony within yourself. Let's explore the gentle world of Tai Chi, a perfect exercise for those who prefer to keep things low-key yet highly beneficial.

Tai Chi is centered around slow, controlled movements combined with deep breathing. This practice focuses on a series of movements called forms. Each form is performed with precision and mindfulness, making Tai Chi an exercise that engages both the mind and the body. The beauty of Tai Chi lies in its simplicity and the minimal space it requires, making it an ideal exercise to start in the comfort of your home. Imagine starting your day with a session of Tai Chi in your living room or backyard, greeting the morning with a sequence that prepares you for the day with calmness and focus.

For those interested in starting Tai Chi, the journey starts with understanding its core principles. Tai Chi movements are slow and deliberate, focusing on fluidity and elegant moves. It's about control rather than speed, about harmony rather than force. Deep breathing is integral, helping to center your thoughts and allowing you to connect deeply with your body. The breath guides the movement, ensuring that physical actions and breath are intertwined. This synchronization enhances lung capacity while also improving mental focus.

Starting at home is surprisingly easy. Many online resources offer beginner-friendly Tai Chi classes and routines. Websites like YouTube have numerous instructional videos that guide you through basic forms. For a more structured approach, consider purchasing DVDs or subscribing to an online tai chi course, where you can follow along with experienced instructors. Set aside a regular time each day for practice, just like you would for any important appointment. This consistency helps you develop a routine and allows the principles of Tai Chi to integrate into your daily life gradually. Make sure your practice space is free from clutter and distractions, creating a sense of peace and readiness for your Tai Chi session.

The benefits of Tai Chi for seniors are profound. Regular practice can significantly improve balance and coordination, reducing the risk of falls, a common concern as we age. The gentle movements strengthen the lower and upper body, enhancing overall muscle tone without strain. Tai Chi also offers excellent cardiovascular benefits, akin to a moderate aerobic workout, but with much lower impact. It's a holistic approach to fitness that fortifies the body, calms the mind, and uplifts the spirit.

Engaging with the Tai Chi community can further enrich your experience. While practicing at home is beneficial, joining a Tai Chi class at a local community center or gym can connect you with others who share your interests. These classes provide guidance under the watchful eye of a skilled instructor and the opportunity to socialize and build new friendships. Taking part in group Tai Chi adds a social dimension to the practice, enhancing the joy and motivation to continue. Many communities also hold Tai Chi events in parks or community spaces, offering a delightful way to practice in nature and meet enthusiasts from all walks of life.

Bringing Tai Chi into your routine is like opening a door to a garden of tranquility where every slow, purposeful movement brings you closer to peace. It's a powerful yet gentle way to enhance your physical health and emotional well-being. As you move in harmony with your breath, each poses a flowing gesture, and you'll find balance in your step and life. So why not give Tai Chi a try? It might be the perfect blend of meditation, movement, and peace you're looking for in your golden years.

Dance Classes: From Salsa to Ballroom

Whoever thinks dancing is just for the youthful crowd hasn't seen the magic and energy in a senior salsa class or the grace of a ballroom dance session tailored for those in the prime time of their lives. Picture yourself swaying to salsa rhythms or gliding across the dance floor during a waltz. It's not just fun; it's a celebration of movement, regardless of age. Let's twirl through the process of choosing a dance style, uncovering the myriad benefits of dancing, and finding the perfect class that makes your heart beat a little faster—literally and metaphorically.

Choosing a dance style is like picking the right spice for your favorite dish; it has to suit your taste and zest for life. If the fiery beats of Latin music stir your soul, salsa might be your dance of choice. Its energetic steps and vibrant music are both exhilarating and incredibly social. On the other hand, if you prefer something more structured, ballroom dancing offers a variety of styles, like the waltz, tango, and foxtrot, each with its unique charm and elegance. The key is to match the dance style with your personality and physical comfort. Don't shy away from trying different styles. Many dance studios offer sample classes where you can try various types before settling on your favorite.

Now, let's cha-cha through the benefits of dancing, and trust me, they extend far beyond just having a good time. Dancing is a fantastic way to improve your physical health. It enhances your strength, coordination, and balance, which are crucial as we age. The varied movements of dance help maintain muscle tone and flexibility, reducing the risk of falls and boosting your overall stamina. But the benefits aren't just physical; dancing offers a mental workout. Remembering steps and sequences boosts brain power and enhances memory. It's like taking your brain to the gym. Moreover, the joy and satisfaction of dancing can significantly uplift your mood, positively impacting your overall mental health. The social aspect of dance classes—meeting new people, enjoying companionship, and perhaps even a little friendly competition—adds to the emotional uplift, combating loneliness and keeping your spirits high.

Finding a suitable dance class might seem daunting, but it's easier than you think. Start by looking for classes specifically designed for seniors or classes that offer a beginner track. It's essential to consider the instructor's experience in teaching older adults. They should be adept at dancing and adapting steps and routines to accommodate varying physical abilities and ensure a safe environment for everyone. Class size also matters; smaller classes provide more personalized attention, which is important when learning new moves. Check local community centers, dance studios, and even fitness clubs; many offer dance classes with skilled instructors who love introducing newcomers to the joys of dancing.

Adjusting dance moves for those with limited mobility or health concerns is critical to ensuring everyone can enjoy the benefits of dancing safely. Instructors skilled in working with seniors can modify steps and routines to meet individual needs. For instance, if balance is a concern, a chair can be used for support during certain moves. The pace can be adjusted to a slower tempo to reduce the risk of strain, and routines can be simplified to focus on upper body movements if someone is not comfortable with vigorous footwork. The goal is to make dance enjoyable and inclusive for everyone, tailoring the experience to allow each participant to thrive within their capabilities.

Dance is not just about the steps or the music; it's a gateway to a joyful and connected life. It's about expressing yourself, meeting new friends, and building confidence in your physical abilities. Whether it's the quick-paced spins of salsa or the swift sweeps of ballroom, each dance style offers a unique way to improve your life, proving that when it comes to dancing, it's never too late to start.

So, lace up your dancing shoes, step into a class, and let the music guide you to a healthier, happier you. Who knows, you might find your feet tapping to the rhythm of joy and your heart dancing to the beat of newfound passions.

Cycling Without Strain: Using E-Bikes

Imagine this:

- You're cruising along a scenic pathway.
- The breeze is gentle.
- The sun is setting.
- You're riding with the ease of a teenager without breaking a sweat.

Welcome to the world of electric bikes, or e-bikes, which are revolutionizing how we think about cycling in our golden years. E-bikes come with a delightful twist; they're equipped with a battery-powered assist that reduces the effort you need to pedal. This means you can cover longer distances, climb hills, and ride with less strain on your body, which can be a game-changer if you love the idea of cycling but are concerned about your stamina or joint health.

E-bikes are your traditional bicycle with a dash of electrical power. Here's how they work: when you pedal, the motor kicks in extra energy to your wheel movement, making accelerating and maintaining speed easier. Some models even come with a throttle, allowing you to enjoy a ride without pedaling—handy for those steep hills! This motor assistance means you can enjoy all the benefits of cycling with less strain, making it a perfect fit for keeping active without overtaxing your body.

Now, let's pedal through the health benefits of cycling on an e-bike. First off, it's a fantastic cardiovascular exercise. Even with motor assistance, you're still pedaling and getting your heart rate up, which is excellent for heart health and boosting overall energy. Cycling also strengthens your legs and lower body muscles, including your thighs, calves, and glutes. And because e-bikes reduce the strain, you can enjoy these benefits without the joint stress that often comes with traditional cycling, making it a kinder option for your knees and hips.

Safety is important when it comes to enjoying your e-bike rides. Always wear a helmet, no matter how short the ride or how safe the route seems. It's your best defense against head injuries. Familiarize yourself with your e-bike's features, especially the power settings and brakes. Knowing how to adjust the motor assistance and stop efficiently can prevent accidents. Also, observe all traffic rules. Just because you're on a bike doesn't mean you can ignore stop signs or red lights. Use bike lanes where available, and always signal your turn to let other road users know your intentions.

For a delightful e-bike experience, seek out scenic routes that are particularly delightful to explore on two wheels. Many communities offer designated bike paths that are away from the hustle and bustle of traffic, allowing you to enjoy nature and the freedom of the open path. Coastal trails, park circuits, or river rides can be exceptionally beautiful and tranquil. Moreover, consider joining a cycling group. Many areas have groups for e-bike riders of all levels. These groups often organize regular rides, which can be an excellent way to meet new people, explore new routes, and keep oneself motivated. Riding with others can turn cycling into a social event filled with laughter and camaraderie, making it something you look forward to each week.

In short, cycling with an e-bike is a superb option for maintaining fitness with joy and ease. It allows you to blend the pleasure of cycling with practical assistance, ensuring a smooth ride regardless of terrain or distance. E-bikes open up a new route to fitness that keeps you active, engaged, and connected with others while enjoying the great outdoors. As we shift gears into the next chapter, remember that every activity we explore offers a unique blend of health benefits and joyous experiences, contributing to a richer, fuller life in retirement. Let's move forward toward the post-retirement wellness and self-care routine, finding new ways to stay active and enjoy every moment of our adventure.

Chapter 3: Wellness and Self-Care

Imagine entering a serene sanctuary where the hustle and bustle of the everyday world melt away, leaving a tranquil harmony in its place. This isn't the latest spa or luxury retreat but rather your own mind, accessible anytime and anywhere through the art of mindfulness and meditation. Who knew retirement could unlock free time and a pathway to profound peace and mental clarity?

Mindfulness and Meditation: Techniques for Peace

Introduction to Mindfulness

At its core, mindfulness is about being fully present in the moment, observing your life unfold one real-time second at a time without judgment or distraction. It's about noticing the world around you, the sensations in your body, and the thoughts crossing your mind. Think of it as being the director of your own mental movie, fully aware of the script, the scenes, and the actors, but choosing not to get lost in the drama. This sense of control over your thoughts and emotions can be incredibly empowering, especially in the golden years of retirement.

Practicing mindfulness can change how you experience everyday life, turning routine activities into moments of deep awareness and appreciation. It's particularly beneficial as we age, helping maintain mental health and emotional balance amidst life's inevitable ups and downs. By creating a greater awareness of the present, mindfulness can reduce stress, enhance relaxation, and a profound sense of contentment—golden qualities in our golden years. These practices can also improve seniors' cognitive function, memory, and overall mental well-being.

Basic Meditation Practices

Meditation, often seen as the formal exercise of mindfulness, involves specific techniques to focus and calm the mind. For those just beginning their journey into meditation, here are a couple of simple practices:

Focused Breathing: This involves concentrating on your breath, an anchor to the present moment. Sit comfortably, close your eyes, and observe the natural rhythm of your breath—inhale and exhale, inhale and exhale. When your mind wanders, gently guide it back to your breath. This practice helps reduce stress and improves lung function, a win-win for mental and physical health.

Guided Imagery: Here, visualization is critical. Picture a serene setting—a quiet beach at sunset, perhaps. Imagine the sights, the sounds, and the smells, immersing yourself in this peaceful scene. Guided imagery is a powerful tool for relaxation and can be particularly soothing during moments of anxiety or stress, transporting you to tranquility.

Integrating Mindfulness into Daily Life

Adding mindfulness into your daily life can be as simple as savoring your morning coffee, truly experiencing the aroma and the warmth, or taking a mindful walk, feeling each step and noting the beauty of your surroundings. The key is consistency and intention. Make a habit of engaging fully with simple daily activities, turning them into mindfulness exercises.

Here's a practical tip: Set regular reminders to pause and practice mindfulness. Use moments like waiting at a red light or during commercials while watching TV as cues to take a few mindful breaths or observe your current thoughts and feelings. With practice, these mindful moments can significantly enhance your awareness and reduce stress, making everyday life more prosperous and enjoyable.

Resources for Deepening Practice

For those looking to deepen their mindfulness and meditation practice, numerous resources are available:

Meditation Apps: Apps like Headspace or Calm offer guided meditation sessions to help structure your practice and explore various meditation techniques.

Books: Consider titles like *Wherever You Go, There You Are* by Jon Kabat-Zinn, a pioneer in mindfulness meditation, or *The Miracle of Mindfulness* by Thich Nhat Hanh, which offers excellent insights into mindfulness practice.

Local Classes: Many community centers, libraries, or wellness centers offer meditation classes that provide guided practice and community support. These classes can be a great way to connect with others who share your wellness journey, fostering a sense of community and reducing feelings of isolation.

By interacting with these resources, you can expand your understanding and practice of mindfulness, making it a more integral part of your life. Whether through apps, books, or community classes, each option offers unique advantages that cater to different learning styles and preferences, enhancing your journey toward mental wellness and emotional balance.

Nutritional Tips for Aging Bodies

As the years tick by, we gain more wisdom and perhaps a few more laugh lines, and our bodies also change how they process food. This shift means that the nutritional needs of folks over 55 take a detour from the younger crowd. Now, it's not just about what tastes good; it's about packing the punch with the right vitamins and minerals without playing a guessing game.

Let's break it down: Our bodies become less efficient at absorbing nutrients as we age. For instance, vitamin B12, crucial for keeping nerves and blood cells healthy, becomes a VIP on your dietary guest list because its absorption decreases with age. Similarly, Calcium steps into the spotlight to maintain those pearly whites and bones, especially as the risk for osteoporosis climbs. And let's not forget vitamin D, notoriously difficult to absorb from sunlight as we age, which helps in calcium absorption and keeps those bones sturdy. Making sure your diet responds to these changes is not just good practice; it's important for keeping you spry and spirited.

Now, maintaining a balanced diet is as difficult as playing a well-tempered symphony. The critical point here is focusing on heart health, bone density, and maintaining those energy levels that might have dipped. Maintaining energy levels is crucial as we age; a balanced diet can help achieve this. A heart-healthy diet is rich in fruits, vegetables, lean proteins, and whole grains. Think Mediterranean diet: olive oil, nuts, and yes, even a glass of red wine can make the cut. Dairy products, green leafy vegetables, and fish like salmon are your go-to allies for bone health. Mix carbohydrates, proteins, and healthy fats throughout the day to keep your energy up. Small, nutrient-dense meals can help maintain energy levels without the burden of heavy digestion that can send you snoozing.

Importance of Hydration

While we're on the subject of a balanced diet, let's pour some attention onto hydration. Water is the unrecognized champion of bodily functions, aiding in everything from digestion to keeping your skin supple. But as we age, our sense of thirst might not be as sharp, tricking us into drinking less water. To keep the waterworks properly flowing, aim for about eight glasses a day, and if plain water doesn't tickle your fancy, add slices of fruits or a splash of juice to flavor it up. Herbal teas are also a great way to hydrate and can be a comforting ritual. Keep a water bottle close by as a visual reminder to sip throughout the day, and consider starting your morning with a glass of water to kickstart your hydration early.

Reading Food Labels

Walking down the grocery store aisles can sometimes feel like being in an episode of a mystery series; what does all this information on food labels mean? Understanding food labels is crucial in making informed choices that align with your health goals. Start with the serving size, found at the top of the label, which sets the stage for understanding the rest of the information. The calories listed refer to the number of calories per serving—not the whole package—so keep that in mind if you're watching your calorie intake.

Next, scan through the nutrients. Aim for foods low in saturated fat, cholesterol, and sodium, which can be villains when it comes to heart health. Fiber, vitamin D, calcium, iron, and potassium, however, are the nutrients you want to invite over more often as they contribute positively to heart health, bone health, and overall vitality. The Percent Daily Value (%DV) gives you a ballpark figure of how much a nutrient in a serving of food contributes to a diet based on 2,000 calories daily. Use this to gauge if a food is high or low in a particular nutrient—5% DV or less is low, and 20% DV or more is high.

By mastering the art of reading food labels, you empower yourself to make choices that nourish your body optimally, aligning with your nutritional needs and health goals. Whether picking the right kind of bread or deciding between two snack options, a little label literacy goes a long way in maintaining your health and zest for life. So, next time you're at the store, take a moment to read those labels—not just for curiosity but for nurturing your body with every bite you take.

Gentle Stretching and Its Benefits

Imagine treating your body like a well-loved book that you want to keep supple and pliable rather than letting it stiffen up on the shelf! That's what stretching does; it keeps your body's pages turning smoothly. As we age, our muscles can become as tight as a drum, which feels uncomfortable and can limit our range of motion. Integrating an excellent old stretch into your routine can be as refreshing as that first-morning coffee. Let's explore how stretching enhances flexibility, reduces muscle tension, and boosts circulation, making you feel like you've just had a tune-up!

Picture this: You're reaching down to tie your shoelaces or picking up that lucky penny off the sidewalk. These simple everyday actions can be smoothly done when your muscles are limber. Regular stretching helps maintain flexibility, which is vital for performing daily activities and preventing injuries. It's similar to oiling the hinges of a squeaky door. The less friction there is, the smoother it moves. Similarly, movements become smoother when your muscles are stretched and cared for, and the risk of muscle cramps and discomfort decreases. Furthermore, stretching helps improve blood circulation, delivering oxygen to your muscles and organs, which is essential for maintaining energy levels and promoting cell growth and healing.

One simple exercise to start with is the seated toe touch. Sit on the edge of a chair with your legs extended. Slowly reach towards your toes, keeping your back straight. This stretch is excellent for your hamstrings and lower back, areas that can be particularly tight. Another great stretch is the chest opener; find a doorway, place your forearms on the door frame, and gently lean forward until you feel a stretch in your chest and shoulders. This is particularly beneficial if you spend a lot of time sitting, as it helps counteract the tendency to hunch over.

For those who enjoy a morning routine or winding down in the evening, consider incorporating stretches like neck rotations and shoulder rolls. These can be done while sitting or standing and help relieve tension that often builds up after long periods of inactivity. Another beneficial stretch is the ankle roll. Lift one foot off the ground, rotate your ankle clockwise, and then counterclockwise. This helps maintain ankle flexibility, which is essential for balance and walking stability.

Stretching into your daily routine doesn't require a gym membership or fancy equipment; it's about using what you have where you are. For instance, while watching your favorite TV show, use the commercial breaks to stand up and do a couple of stretches. Or implement a morning ritual where you spend a few minutes stretching before breakfast. It's about making stretching a natural part of your day so that it doesn't feel like a chore but a refreshing part of your lifestyle.

Safety, of course, comes first when it comes to stretching. Stretching gently and within your comfort zone is vital to avoid injuries. Always warm up a little before you begin stretching. This can be as simple as walking in place for a few minutes to get the blood flowing. Refrain from forcing a stretch beyond what feels comfortable. Stretching should never cause pain. If you feel pain, ease up and consider consulting a professional like a physical therapist who can guide you on stretching properly and safely. They can provide personalized stretches that cater specifically to your body's needs.

Regular stretching is like whispering sweet nothings to your muscles; they respond by keeping you flexible, active, and ready to bend without breaking. So, whether you're reaching for a book on the top shelf or swinging a golf club, those stretches you've woven into your daily routine are the unsung heroes behind your ability to move easily and confidently. Keep stretching and keep moving, and watch how your body thanks you in countless ways. From improved mobility to a better quality of life, the benefits will be evident.

Stress Management Techniques for Seniors

Stress, that sneaky little gremlin, doesn't retire when you do. In fact, it might just be more bothersome when you thought you'd be sipping lemonade on the porch without a care in the world. But do not worry; recognizing what cranks up your stress is the first step towards managing it and turning those potential frowns upside down. Identifying your personal stress triggers can be quite an eye-opener. It could be anything from financial concerns, health troubles, or even the daily headlines. Once you've identified these triggers, you can take steps to reduce and manage them more effectively. Keeping a stress diary can be exceptionally revealing. Note when you feel stressed, what's happening, and how you respond. This isn't just busywork; it's your personal detective kit for uncovering patterns and solutions that work uniquely for you.

Now, let's talk about melting that stress away. Ever tried progressive muscle relaxation? It's like giving your body a good night's kiss, preparing it for sweet dreams. Here it goes: You tense each muscle group vigorously without straining. Release the tension suddenly and feel the muscles relax. Start from your toes and work your way up to your head. It's an effective way to release stress and a satisfying end to a long day. Deep breathing exercises are another treasure. Focusing on deep, steady breaths might help you relax and lessen anxiety. Picture your belly as a balloon, inflating as you breathe in, deflating as you breathe out; simple yet profoundly calming.

Creating a calming environment at home plays an important role in stress management. Start by decluttering your space. A cluttered space can lead to a cluttered mind, and who needs that? Opt for colors that soothe the soul—soft blues, greens, and lavenders are like a visual spa treatment. Consider adding some plants; they're beautiful to look at and improve air quality. And let's not forget the power of a good scent. Aromatherapy can work wonders: lavender for relaxation, peppermint to invigorate, and perhaps rosemary to improve focus. Create a small space in your home where you may retreat when you need a break from the tension. Fill it with cozy cushions, maybe add a small fountain for the soothing sounds of water, and voila, you have a stress-free sanctuary!

However, sometimes stress can feel bigger than what home remedies can soothe. If you find stress overwhelming your life, it might be time to seek professional help. There's no shame in it; think of it as outsourcing for your well-being. Counseling or therapy can provide you with effective strategies to manage stress and cope with life's challenges. Many therapists now offer sessions online, allowing you to find support from the comfort of your own home. If you're unsure where to start, your doctor can provide a referral. Remember, asking for help is a sign of strength, not weakness. In managing stress, just like in many other areas of life, it often takes a village, and there's plenty of help out there to ensure you continue to enjoy your retirement years with the peace and joy you deserve.

Essential Routines for Daily Wellness

Picture this: The sun just peeking over the horizon, a fresh page in your journal, and a day yours for the taking. Ah, the sweet symphony of a morning routine that sets the tone for a harmonious day. Consider incorporating routines that are uplifting and supportive of your well-being from the moment you get up. Believe it or not, morning routines can be your secret weapon for a fruitful day ahead. Let's start with a light exercise; nothing says "good morning" to your body like a gentle stretch or a brisk walk around the block. It wakes up your muscles, gets that blood flowing, and infuses energy that can carry you through the day. Next up, how about immersing yourself in a book or scribbling down your thoughts in a journal? This isn't just about leisure; it's about setting a calm, reflective tone for the day, giving you a quiet moment to pour your thoughts out or get lost in a story before the day ramps up.

Let's talk about the cornerstone of good health—sleep. Good sleep hygiene isn't just about catching zzz but making sure they are quality zzz. Establishing a regular sleep schedule creates a rhythm for your body's internal clock, which can help you fall asleep and wake up more naturally. Think about it: Going to bed and waking up at the same time every day turns sleep into a reliable friend rather than a fickle acquaintance. But the environment matters too. Your bedroom should be a sanctuary for sleep, so invest in comfortable bedding and use light-blocking curtains to keep it dark. If outside sounds are a nuisance, consider using a white noise machine. Keep gadgets out of the bedroom; that means parting with your smartphone and TV at bedtime. The blue light emitted can interfere with your ability to fall asleep. Instead, why not create a bedtime ritual? Perhaps a warm bath, a cup of herbal tea, or a few minutes of reading something light to help your body wind down.

Now, let's make a summary of your social activities in a day. Regular social activities are not just fun; they are a lifeline to mental health, providing emotional support, reducing stress, and warding off loneliness. Integrating these activities into your daily life can be as simple as scheduling regular coffee dates with friends or joining a club or class that meets regularly. These aren't just social appointments; they're checkpoints that keep you engaged, connected, and mentally active. In today's digital age, staying social doesn't always mean stepping out. Video calls, social media, and even old-fashioned phone calls can keep you linked to your social circle, allowing you to share laughs, swap stories, and maintain those vital connections no matter where you are.

Lastly, let's touch on a tool that's as insightful as it is simple—a mood diary. Keeping track of your mental health can sometimes be as easy as jotting down a few notes on your emotional ups and downs throughout the day. This practice helps you recognize patterns or triggers in your mood and provides a way to express feelings safely. Additionally, it can be a valuable tool for communicating your mental state with healthcare providers. To complement your mood diary, consider using mental health apps that can help track your emotions, offer meditation or breathing exercises, and provide resources for managing stress and anxiety. These apps are like having a mini-therapist in your pocket, ready to support you with tools and tips no matter where you are or how you feel.

While adding these routines to your daily life, you have boosted yourself up with rich wellness, preparedness, and emotional clarity. From the moment you open your eyes to the world to the minute you drift back into sleep, each routine plays a crucial role in maintaining your physical health and your zest for life. So, why not give these routines a shot? They might just turn every day into a good day—or at least a better one!

The Importance of Regular Check-ups and Health Monitoring

Let's face it; none of us are as young as we used to be, and as the years pile on, so does the need for a bit more maintenance to keep this well-oiled machine we call our body running smoothly. Regular medical check-ups and screenings might not be the most exhilarating of activities, but think of them as your personal tune-up sessions— vital for catching any sneaky issues before they become major headaches. It's a bit like taking your car in for an oil change to keep everything running without a hitch, but in this case, it's about keeping you in top-notch condition.

Scheduling these health appointments regularly is a cornerstone of preventive healthcare. Just like you wouldn't wait for your car to break down before servicing it, treating your health the same way can prevent many common issues that tend to crop up in our senior years. Early detection of conditions like hypertension, diabetes, or heart disease can make a significant difference in treatment success. Not to add that detecting things early frequently results in simpler, less invasive therapies, which who wouldn't prefer? Schedule appointments with your primary care physician, eye doctor, and other specialists as a regular occurrence, just as you would for birthdays and anniversaries. This regular rhythm keeps you informed about your health status. It builds a valuable ongoing relationship with your healthcare providers.

Now, on to something equally important: keeping track of your medical history. It's like having a detailed logbook of every service and repair your car has had, only this one's about you. Maintaining an up-to-date record of your vaccinations, past treatments, and ongoing health conditions isn't just about good housekeeping. It's crucial for effective healthcare. This record should be comprehensive, containing details about your medical operations or hospital visits, as well as a list of drugs, allergies, and even family-inherited problems. Why? Because every piece of this puzzle helps your healthcare provider see the complete picture, leading to better, more personalized care. Keeping a copy of this record at home and even a version on your phone is a good idea; digital health apps can be great for this. That way, if you ever need to visit a new specialist or require emergency care, everything they need to know is at their fingertips.

Understanding health metrics like blood pressure, cholesterol, and blood sugar levels is not just for medical professionals. Getting to grips with what these numbers mean can empower you to manage your health proactively. For instance, knowing that your blood pressure is in a healthy range or your cholesterol levels are high can motivate you to make dietary changes or stick to your medication schedule. Think of these metrics as the dashboard indicators on your car. If a light flashes, it's telling you that something needs attention. Similarly, if your blood sugar levels are consistently high, it's time to consult your doctor and perhaps make some lifestyle adjustments.

Leveraging technology can make monitoring these health metrics a breeze. Wearable devices like fitness trackers and smartwatches are more than just fancy gadgets for the younger crowd. They can be a game-changer for seniors by keeping track of heart rates, activity levels, and even sleep patterns. Many of these gadgets may link with smartphone apps to provide a comprehensive view of your health data. This continuous monitoring can provide insights that might go unnoticed during occasional doctor visits, allowing for timely interventions. Plus, they can add a layer of fun to maintaining your health; competing with yourself to get more steps each day or improve your heart rate can be a pretty engaging challenge.

So, as we are wrapping up, remember that taking proactive steps in monitoring and maintaining your health can make all the difference. Regular check-ups, an updated medical history, understanding your health metrics, and using technology can keep you surviving and thriving. As you move on to the next chapter and start your own book club, fulfilling a long-held dream, carry with you a commitment to treat your health as you would any valuable asset. Care for it diligently and proudly, knowing it's what allows you to enjoy the rich, vibrant life you lead. Remember, maintaining your well-being is key to making the most of every moment and opportunity.

Chapter 4: Engaging the Mind

The mind! That wondrous playground where thoughts frolic and ideas take flight. As you stroll into the lush landscape of retirement, what better way to adorn your days than by peppering them with activities that tickle your intellect and stir your soul? Using your intellect is more than just staying sharp; it's about broadening your horizons beyond the comfort of your favorite reading nook or the energetic bustle of a neighborhood café. In this chapter, we'll unwrap the delightful world of reading and the communal joy of book clubs, where stories leap off the page and conversations spark deeper connections.

The Pleasure of Reading: Starting a Book Club

Choosing the Right Books

Picture this: a group of friends, each with a book in hand, animatedly discussing a character's fate or the plot twist. Starting a book club is like throwing a dinner party where the dishes are made of paper and ink; every course is a different genre. The key ingredient? Choosing the right books. You'll want a menu that appeals to various palates, stirring up interest and inviting spirited discussions. Explore a variety of genres, such as a heartfelt historical tale, a spicy mystery, or a lighthearted comedy. Include novels that question and provoke, providing fresh ideas and compelling stories. Why not pick a book that travels through exotic locales or one that tackles a slice of history? The diversity of selections keeps the discussions vibrant and the pages turning. Don't shy away from new or lesser-known authors; sometimes, the most engaging conversations come from unexpected sources. And remember, the best books are not always the ones everyone likes, but the ones that get everyone talking.

Organizing the Club

Now, how does one go about orchestrating this literary symphony? Organizing a book club is less about bureaucracy and more about camaraderie. Start by gathering your fellow readers, friends, neighbors, or even new acquaintances who share your zest for reading. Decide how often you'll meet; once a month is a comfortable pace that gives everyone time to read the book without rushing. When it comes to the meeting place, rotate among members' homes or pick a cozy spot in a local café or library. Set a consistent schedule, and consider creating a basic online calendar to keep track of your gatherings. During your meetings, appoint a discussion leader for each book, someone who can steer the conversation, ensuring everyone gets a chance to voice their thoughts. This role can rotate with each book, allowing all members to guide the discussion.

Enhancing Discussions

To spice up your book club discussions, arrive armed with more than just your opinions. Preparing a few thought-provoking questions in advance can help jumpstart conversations and uncover layers of the story that might otherwise go unnoticed. Encourage members to bring their own questions or insights, fostering a richer exchange of ideas. Discuss not just the plot and characters but also the themes, the writing style, and how the book relates to modern times or personal experiences. Embrace diverse viewpoints; the beauty of a book club lies in seeing through the eyes of others, which can often reveal new insights about the book and each other.

Expanding Horizons

Lastly, let your book club be a vessel for broader exploration. Use books as gateways to learn about different cultures, historical periods, or philosophical ideas. Perhaps complement a novel set in India with a night of Indian cuisine, or follow a book about a famous painter by organizing a group visit to an art gallery. This enriches your understanding of the book and enhances the social experience, making each meeting something to look forward to. Books can transport us not only to different worlds but also into the minds and hearts of people different from ourselves, broadening our horizons and understanding of the world.

Reading and discussing is an excellent method to keep your mind active and the conversation going. A book club combines the joy of discovery with the warmth of community, creating a space where literature meets life, and every page becomes a new opportunity for connection and growth. So gather your friends, pick a book, and let the discussions—and the wine—flow. Who knows what new adventures await in the chapters to come?

Puzzle Fun: Crosswords and Sudoku

The humble crossword and its numerical cousin, Sudoku, aren't just idle pastimes but gateways to keeping your mind as sharp as a tack. Who would have thought that filling out a few squares could be akin to lifting weights for your brain? Let me tell you, whether it's a word or a number puzzle, each one you conquer boosts your mood and flexes those mental muscles. It's like a daily brain exercise that prevents cognitive rust, improves problem-solving abilities, and strengthens memory.

Now, you might wonder, how exactly do these puzzles help? When you sit down with a crossword, you're not just hunting for words; you're diving into a mental exercise that requires you to recall vocabulary, general knowledge, and sometimes even a bit of trivia. This process is fantastic for memory retention. With its grids and numbers, Sudoku challenges your logical reasoning and pattern recognition skills. Regular engagement with these puzzles can help enhance your focus and concentration, keeping your mind engaged and active. It's like holding your brain in a lively dance of neurons, ensuring it stays vibrant and agile.

Finding these puzzles is as easy as pie. Your daily newspaper is a treasure trove of fresh crosswords and Sudoku puzzles. The internet is brimming with resources for those who prefer a digital touch. Websites like New York Times Crossword, Washington Post Crossword, and Sudoku.com offer a plethora of puzzles ranging from the blissfully simple to the devilishly difficult. These platforms frequently allow you to select your level of difficulty, so whether you're a beginner or a seasoned puzzler, you may find something to suit your mood and ability level. And let's not forget apps, downloadable directly to your smartphone or tablet; these apps ensure you have a puzzle handy whenever the mood strikes, be it during a quiet moment at home or while sitting on a park bench on a sunny afternoon.

Puzzle-solving would be a healthier addition to your daily routine. It can be as refreshing as your morning cup of coffee. Start your day with a crossword at breakfast, or unwind in the evening with a Sudoku puzzle. Make it a part of your daily "me-time," a way to relax and recharge. You could also set a puzzle date with yourself, dedicating specific times in your week to dive into more challenging puzzles. This gives you something exciting to look forward to and establishes a healthy, stimulating routine.

Now, for a twist of creativity: How about crafting your own puzzles? Imagine the delight of creating a crossword where the clues lead to memories shared with friends and family or designing a Sudoku puzzle that you can challenge your spouse or grandchildren with. Creating puzzles can be a profoundly satisfying experience; it's a fun way to express your creativity and a great exercise in cognitive skills. Tools like Crossword Hobbyist or Armored Penguin make the process easy, allowing you to create professional-looking puzzles.

Imagine the next family gathering where you pull out a crossword all about family trivia—what a hoot that would be! It's a great opportunity to participate, connect, and have some fun while also exercising your brain.

So, whether you're solving the wordplay in a crossword or lining up numbers in Sudoku, remember, every puzzle solved is like a high-five to your brain. It's about pushing the boundaries of your cognitive abilities, one square at a time, keeping your mind agile and ready to tackle whatever comes next. Grab that pencil, get those neurons firing, and let the puzzling fun begin!

Lifelong Learning: Online Courses for Seniors

The digital age offers an abundance of learning opportunities that combine the ease of learning from home. Imagine mastering Italian cooking while in your pajamas or unraveling the mysteries of the stars through an online astronomy course. Online learning platforms like Coursera, Udemy, and Khan Academy are your gateways to this vibrant world of knowledge. These platforms offer courses on virtually everything under the sun, taught by experts from around the globe. Whether you're looking to dabble in digital photography, get a grip on classical music theory, or dive deep into the realms of history, these platforms have you covered.

Exploring these platforms is like walking through a well-organized library. Prerequisites, user evaluations, and thorough descriptions are usually included with each course listing to assist you in determining the course's suitability and relevance. Most platforms allow you to search by subject, difficulty level, or even by specific instructors. Coursera and Udemy, for example, offer user-friendly interfaces where signing up is as easy as creating an account and clicking "enroll." And let's not forget the previews! Much like flipping through a book in a bookstore, most courses offer preview videos or a syllabus so you can get a taste of the course content before committing.

Choosing the right course can sometimes feel like finding the right book in a vast library. Start by aligning your course choice with your personal interests or something you've always wanted to learn but never had the time for. However, it's also beneficial to step out of your comfort zone occasionally. If you're traditionally a history buff, why not try a basic coding class? The idea is to balance enjoyment with challenge. Consider also the practical applications. For instance, a course in personal finance management can offer skills you can use every day. The key is to choose classes that interest you and add value to your daily life, providing skills you can apply in real-world situations.

Viewing the course videos is not the end of the engagement. The majority of platforms have discussion groups or forums where you may talk with students from all over the world. These forums are gold mines for enriching your learning experience. Pose questions, share insights, or even find study buddies. For those who relish real-time interaction, some platforms offer live webinars or Q&A sessions with instructors. This interaction makes the learning process more dynamic and less isolated, giving you a classroom feel.

Maintaining your motivation can sometimes be the trickiest part of online learning. Setting realistic and clear-cut goals is crucial. You may aim to complete a four-week course over two months or decide to dedicate two hours a week to learning. Mark your progress on a calendar or set reminders. Enjoy the little things in life. Completing a difficult subject or getting a decent grade on an exam can feel great. Remember, the flexibility of online learning means you can tailor the pace to suit your lifestyle, so set a pace that challenges yet accommodates you comfortably without overwhelming you.

Every click in the huge world of online education pulls you closer to new abilities and information. This helps you grow from a mere student of a subject into a lifelong student of the great mysteries of the universe. So, why wait? Sign up for that course you've been eyeing, dive into learning new skills, and perhaps discover a hidden passion. With every lesson and every interaction, you grow not just in knowledge but as a vibrant, engaged member of your community, continually evolving and embracing the joy of learning.

Writing Your Memoirs: A Guide to Telling Your Story

Ah, memoir writing! It's similar to having someone around for a cup of tea in your living room and sharing with them the stories of your life, including the adventures, the turning points, and even the seemingly ordinary yet subtly magical everyday events. Writing your memoirs isn't just about documenting events; it's about sharing the essence of your life's journey, the wisdom gained, and the laughs you had along the way. It's a lovely way to leave a lasting legacy and possibly inspire and educate others—including future generations who might be curious about the kind of life you lead.

Starting this delightful endeavor can seem a bit daunting at first—after all, you've got a lifetime of stories! But fear not. Begin by jotting down memories as they come to you without worrying about chronology or making sense just yet. Think of it as a brainstorming session where every memory, whether it's your fifth birthday party or that impromptu road trip in your twenties, gets a moment in the spotlight. Memory triggers can be really useful here. Old images, cherished music, and even the aroma of perfume can evoke a flood of recollections. Keep a notebook or a digital document nearby to record these glimpses of the past as they occur. Once you have a good collection, start organizing these memories into a timeline. It's like arranging a puzzle; you know all the pieces need to fit together in a coherent way that tells your story.

Now, let's explore tools because even the most skilled carpenter can't build a house without a hammer and nails. In the world of writing, your tools will include everything from basic word processors like Microsoft Word to more specialized writing software like Scrivener, which is fantastic for organizing large projects like memoirs. Scrivener allows you to keep notes, research, and your manuscript all in one place, and you can easily rearrange sections as your work progresses. For those who might feel a bit intimidated by new software, don't worry. Many of these programs offer tutorials to get you started.

Additionally, online workshops can be invaluable. Websites like MasterClass or The Memoir Academy offer sessions with experienced writers who can guide you through the process of shaping your narratives. Local writing groups are also a goldmine for getting feedback and encouragement. Sharing your work with others can be intimidating, but it's also a great way to learn new things and enhance your writing.

Preserving personal histories is not just about leaving a legacy; it's about capturing the emotions and experiences that have shaped who you are. The stories you choose to tell are pieces of a puzzle that together create a portrait of your life. They can provide joy, inspiration, and even healing to anyone who reads them. Consider what you want to leave behind, including lessons and chuckles, and let that influence your writing. Remember, every life is an incredible story worth telling, and your unique perspective is what will make your memoir resonate with readers.

Exploring publishing options can turn these personal reflections into a book that sits on shelves, including your own. The world of publishing has expanded dramatically with the advent of digital platforms. Self-publishing on platforms like Amazon's Kindle Direct Publishing lets you control the entire process, from design to distribution, and it's a fantastic option for getting your story out into the world quickly. While more challenging to break into, traditional publishing can offer the advantage of professional editing and broader distribution. Consider your memoir goals: will you share it with relatives and friends, or do you want to reach a larger audience? The answers to these questions will have a huge impact on your publishing career path.

The Art of Pottery: Shaping Clay Into Memories

Pottery-Indeed a timeless art! There's something almost magical about taking a lump of clay and transforming it into a piece that's both functional and beautiful, a vessel that holds not just food or flowers but also a piece of your soul. If you've ever felt the call to create, to get your hands a little dirty and really make something from scratch, pottery might just be the perfect craft for you. It's not only profoundly satisfying to mold and shape clay with your own hands, but it's also wonderfully therapeutic.

Let's start with a beginner's guide to this delightful craft. Pottery primarily involves two basic techniques: wheel throwing and hand-building. You often see wheel throwing in movies—clay spinning on a wheel while you shape it with your hands. It's mesmerizing to watch and even more enchanting to try. Hand-building, on the other hand, is easier for beginners to learn and does not require a wheel. Hand-building includes techniques like pinching, coiling, and slab construction, which may be completed with only a few tools and your bare hands. Both methods have their charms, and both offer endless possibilities for creativity.

Finding the right class can lead you to a fulfilling pottery adventure. Many community centers, art schools, and even some colleges offer pottery classes that cater to different skill levels. When searching for a class, look for one that welcomes beginners and possibly focuses on seniors. These workshops are more likely to provide a speed and style of instruction that is appropriate for people who may require more time to get into the swing of things or who want a gentler approach to learning this art. Some studios even offer trial sessions so you may acquire a feel for pottery before committing to a full course right away. This can be a fantastic way to dip your toes into the muddy waters of pottery without diving in headfirst.

The therapeutic benefits of working with clay are well-documented and profound. There's a soothing, almost meditative quality to the way clay moves in your hands. As you focus on molding and shaping, the world's worries fade away, leaving you in a tranquil state of mind. This kind of focus can help reduce stress and promote a sense of well-being. Moreover, the tactile nature of clay can be a sensory delight, which stimulates your brain in a way that many other hobbies do not. The act of creating something tangible is incredibly rewarding; it's a process that can give you a strong sense of accomplishment and pride.

For those just starting out, it's wise to begin with some simple projects. Perhaps a small pinch pot or a simple coil cup. These projects don't require much equipment and offer a great way to get familiar with the texture and behavior of clay. As your confidence improves, you may go to more intricate forms like plates, bowls, or even ornamental vases. Whether small or basic, each piece you make displays your imagination and represents a step forward in your pottery journey.

Pottery is more than just a hobby; it's a skill you can hone over a lifetime, and each piece you make is a snapshot of your creative journey. Whether spinning the wheel or building by hand, each method brings joy and challenges, making pottery a deeply enriching way to express yourself. So, why not give it a spin? Get your hands dirty, let your creative juices flow, and shape some beautiful memories out of clay. Who knows? Your next masterpiece could be just a lump of clay away.

Bird Watching: Discovering Nature's Beauty

Bird watching is not just about spotting a rare species or ticking off numbers on a list; it's about the quiet thrill of connecting with nature and the joy of discovering the diverse tapestry of avian life that flutters around us. Whether peering through a pair of binoculars at a park or just observing the visitors to your backyard feeder, bird watching can be a surprisingly engaging and utterly serene way to spend your time.

Let's start with the basics: You'll need a good pair of binoculars to get into bird watching. Think of them as your passport to the world of birds, a tool that brings distant beauties into clear view. When choosing binoculars, look for something lightweight with a comfortable grip and good magnification—8x to 10x is usually sufficient. The objective lens diameter (the second number in binocular specs, like 8 x 42) is also crucial; a larger lens (around 40-42 mm) is ideal as it allows more light, making your view brighter and clearer. Now, spotting and identifying birds is like learning to appreciate fine art; the more you do it, the better you get. Begin with a field guide that lists the bird species in your area. These guides identify species using descriptions, photographs, or illustrations and provide information on behavior, vocalizations, and habitats. Apps like Merlin Bird ID and Audubon Bird Guide are fantastic digital companions, offering real-time tools to identify and learn about birds.

The benefits of bird watching extend far beyond the pleasure of identification. For many, it becomes a meditative practice; the focus required to spot and identify birds allows you to tune out distractions and immerse yourself fully in the moment. This focused observation can greatly reduce stress and improve your general mental health. Physically, bird viewing frequently entails treks or hikes, which are an excellent way to get some light, pleasurable exercise. Moreover, the connection to nature that comes from observing birds can deepen your appreciation for the natural world, fostering a sense of environmental stewardship and a desire to conserve these wonderful creatures and their habitats.

Participating in local bird-watching groups or events can amplify these benefits. Most communities have birding clubs that organize regular outings, which can be a wonderful way to meet like-minded individuals and learn from more experienced birders. These groups often participate in bird counts or other citizen science projects, which can be incredibly rewarding; you're not just watching birds but contributing to their conservation. Check local nature centers, wildlife organizations, or online platforms like Meetup to find a bird-watching group near you.

Documenting your bird sightings adds another layer of enjoyment to this hobby. Keeping a bird journal or using an app to log your sightings can help you track your progress as a birder, and over time, you'll build a personal archive that reflects your growth and the seasons of the avian world. Apps like eBird allow you to record your sightings and share them with a global community of birders, providing essential data that helps scientists monitor bird populations and trends. This practice enhances your bird-watching experience and connects you to a larger purpose, as each entry you make is a small piece of a much bigger conservation puzzle.

Bird watching is a gentle yet immensely satisfying way to engage with the natural world. It requires little more than patience and curiosity, yet it offers back so much in terms of relaxation, knowledge, and connection. As you spend more time with your feathered neighbors, you'll notice that each bird song and wing flutter instills a greater appreciation for nature's complexities and fragile beauty. So, grab your binoculars and a field guide, step outside, and let the birds guide you to a more mindful, joyful day. Who knows what feathered wonders await your discovery?

As we wrap up this vibrant chapter on engaging the mind, remember that each activity, from the intellectual stimulation of book clubs and puzzles to the creative expression of pottery and the tranquil pursuit of bird watching, is not just a pastime but a portal to new learning and experiences. These activities enrich your days, broaden your horizons, and connect you with communities and passions that invigorate your life. Stepping into the next chapter, we'll explore how these enriched social experiences enhance personal joy and contribute to a balanced, vibrant lifestyle filled with friends and new social experiences in your golden years. Let's continue this delightful exploration, shall we?

Chapter 5: Building and Maintaining Social Connections

Retirement is a time when the calendar pages flip from meetings and deadlines to opportunities for leisure and volunteering. If you've ever thought retirement might mean a quieter, perhaps lonelier life, think again! It's actually the perfect time to weave new social tapestries, and what better thread to use than the rich, rewarding experiences of volunteering? Volunteering, whether at the local library, planting trees, or providing meals to those in need, is more than just giving back; it's a golden ticket to feeling more connected to your community and making new friends who share your passion for good.

Volunteering: Giving Back to Feel Connected

Identifying Opportunities

So, where do you begin in this noble pursuit? First, let's find the right fit for your interests and abilities. Start local; community centers, hospitals, and schools often need volunteers for various roles, from mentoring young minds to brightening the days of hospital patients with friendly visits. Don't forget about environmental organizations or animal shelters, where you may assist protect local wildlife or hug cats and dogs in need. A simple visit to a local nonprofit's website or a conversation with friends who participate in community events can lead to these chances. Websites like VolunteerMatch.org are also fantastic resources, allowing you to search for volunteer opportunities based on your interests and location. Imagine the satisfaction of aligning your passion for books with volunteering at the library's next book sale!

Benefits of Volunteering

Now, let's talk about perks because there are many! Volunteering connects you to others, making it a fantastic antidote to the isolation that can sometimes sneak into our golden years. It's about more than just the tasks at hand; it's about contributing to a community that values your presence and skills, boosting your self-esteem and sense of purpose. Studies show that engaging in volunteer work can significantly lower depression and loneliness, which are as detrimental to health as smoking or obesity. There's something deeply satisfying about being a part of something bigger than yourself and seeing the direct impact of your generosity on the lives of people and the community. This sense of fulfillment and purpose is a powerful motivator for retirees, making them feel valued and integral to their communities.

Adapting to Physical Limitations

What if your eagerness is willing, but your knees are not? No worries! Volunteering doesn't have to be physically demanding. Many roles need your wisdom more than your physical strength. Administrative tasks, tutoring, or crafting from home can be as impactful. Communicate openly about any physical limitations you might have with the organization; most are more than willing to accommodate volunteers of all abilities because your time and heart genuinely matter.

Making Social Connections Through Volunteering

One of the most delightful surprises in volunteering is the friendships it can foster. Shared activities create common ground; working alongside others towards a common goal naturally promotes connections. These aren't just fellow volunteers but potential friends who share your values and interests. Whether you're wrapping books at the library fundraiser or walking dogs at the shelter, each activity offers a chance to chat, share stories, and build bonds. Over time, these ties strengthen, widening your social network and enhancing your life with helpful, like-minded people. The delight of making new acquaintances through volunteering might help seniors feel enthusiastic about their social prospects. Imagine heading to a volunteer event and being greeted by familiar faces, all ready to join forces and make a difference; it's like being part of a special club where everyone wins.

Volunteering in retirement opens up a world of opportunities to stay active, engaged, and connected. It's about putting your skills, expertise, and enthusiasm to good use while also expanding your social life and making a real difference in your community. So, why not step out and try it? The rewards are bound to be more than you give.

Joining Local Clubs and Societies

Now, isn't it a joy to think that somewhere out there, a group of like-minded folks is gathering to share their passions, whether gardening, reading, or snapping the perfect photograph? Joining a local club or society can be more than just a leisure activity; it's a doorway to community involvement, enriched social interactions, and a lot of fun. Whether you're a green-thumbed gardener looking to share your love of orchids or a literary aficionado looking for others who understand the nuances of Nabokov, there's probably a club out there with members who share your passion.

Let's start by explaining how to find these clubs. Your local community center or library is a treasure trove of information about clubs and societies in your area. Often, they'll have notice boards filled with flyers or can provide a calendar of meet-ups. The internet is also your friend here. A fast search for phrases like "photography club [your city]" or "book club near me" can turn up a surprisingly large number of results. For this reason, websites such as Meetup.com are great since they group people according to interests, so you can get very involved in any pastime you're interested in, like knitting or kayaking.

Once you've found a club that sparks your interest, active participation is the key to making the most of it. Don't just be a name on the membership list; dive into the activities. Attend meetings regularly, participate in discussions, volunteer for organizing events, or share your ideas for new projects. Active involvement enriches the experience and opens up more opportunities for deeper connections with fellow members. Active participation in organizations and societies can provide retirees with a sense of belonging, making them feel included and part of a community. Remember, the energy you invest in the club is often directly proportional to what you get out of it, both in terms of enjoyment and social interaction.

But what if no club in your area matches your interests? Why not start your own? It might sound daunting, but with a sprinkle of initiative and a dash of organization, you can bring together a group of people who share your interests. Start by defining the purpose and goals of your club. What will be the focus? Who would be interested? Once you have a clear vision, spread the word. Use social media, community bulletin boards, or even local newspapers to reach out to potential members. Organize an initial meeting in a public area, such as a coffee shop or a library room, to create a comfortable mood for this first gathering.

The benefits of being part of a club extend far beyond the activities themselves. Regular meetings provide a consistent social schedule that can structure your week and give you something exciting to look forward to. Shared experiences—be it a book discussion that turned surprisingly profound or a group trip to a local botanical garden— foster a sense of belonging and can significantly enhance your social life. Over time, these club members can become a support network, people you can turn to for advice on your hobby and companionship and support in your day-to-day life.

So, consider this your invitation to step out and explore the clubs and societies your community offers. Whether you're meeting to discuss the latest bestseller or to share gardening tips, each meeting enriches your life, expands your horizons, and ties you closer to your community. It's about forming a network of friends and fellow enthusiasts who share your passions and interests so that every club gathering is more than simply an event but also a celebration of shared interests and new friendships. What are you waiting for? Your new club members are just around the corner, waiting to meet you!

How to Start a Social Group in Your Community

Imagine you've just discovered a fantastic new hobby, or perhaps you've noticed a gap in your community's social offerings; maybe it's a need for a film appreciation club, a group for amateur astronomers, or even a social circle for fellow retirees interested in local history. Whatever your specialization, forming a new social club can help you enrich your social life while also serving as a useful resource for your community. Let's put on our event organizer hats and dive into how you can bring people together around a shared interest, creating a vibrant, engaging community group from scratch.

First, how do you determine what kind of group might thrive in your area? Start by playing detective in your community. Attend local events, chat with neighbors, or participate in forums to gauge interests and uncover unmet needs. Local community centers often have bulletin boards featuring upcoming events, which can provide insights into what's already happening and what's missing. For instance, if you notice a recurring theme of health and wellness events but nothing in the way of cultural activities like a book club or a film group, there's your niche! Conducting informal surveys can also be a great tool; simple questions like "What hobbies interest you?" or "What kind of group would you join if it were available?" can yield valuable information that helps tailor your group to community interests.

Now that you've pinpointed a potential focus for your group, let's talk logistics. Planning and organization are crucial to transforming your idea into a thriving social group. Begin by establishing the group's purpose and objectives; this will influence all of your decisions, from the activities you plan to who you invite. Next, consider the structure: Will it be more casual, with open membership, or will it require registration to keep numbers manageable? Finding a meeting place is crucial; local libraries, community centers, and even cafes can be excellent venues, depending on the nature of the group. Establishing a regular schedule—whether weekly, bi-weekly, or monthly—helps members make your group a recurring part of their routine. In the initial stages, planning the first few sessions with specific activities or discussions might help get the ball rolling and encourage active participation.

Promoting your group is next on the agenda. You want to make some noise—well, the good kind—to get people excited and involved. Creating eye-catching flyers to post at community centers, libraries, and grocery stores can capture interest. Social media is also a powerful tool for reaching a wider audience. Platforms like Facebook and Instagram allow you to create event pages, share updates, and invite local community members. Don't underestimate the power of word-of-mouth; encourage friends and acquaintances to spread the word. The more personal and relevant your campaign appears, the more likely it is to appeal to potential members.

Keeping the group active and engaged is crucial for long-term success. One effective strategy is rotating leadership roles. This distributes the workload and gives members a sense of ownership and involvement in the group's direction. Continuously providing new activities or discussion topics keeps the group lively and prevents it from getting stagnant. For example, suppose you've started a gardening club. In that case, you might rotate topics from practical gardening tips in one meeting to a discussion on sustainable practices the next or even organize a plant swap. Regular feedback from members about what they enjoy or want more of can also guide the evolution of the group, ensuring it remains relevant and engaging.

Starting a social group in your community is a wonderful way to meet people, explore interests, and contribute to the vibrancy of your local area. It's about more than just shared hobbies; it's about crafting a space where people can connect, learn, and grow together. Whether you're rallying film buffs for a monthly movie night or gathering culinary enthusiasts for a potluck of international dishes, the group you create could become a cherished part of someone's social life, including yours. So, take that leap, gather your community, and watch your idea blossom into a thriving group. Who knows, the connections you foster might turn into lifelong friendships starting from one shared interest.

Using Social Media to Stay Connected with Family and Friends

Social media is like the town square of yesteryear but in the digital age. Whether you're sharing images from your recent vacation or keeping up with family news, platforms like Facebook, Instagram, and Twitter may help you stay in touch with your loved ones. But I hear you ask, "How do I navigate these digital streets?" Let's demystify these platforms, ensuring you can chat and share with the best of them while keeping your digital self safe and sound.

First things first, setting up your accounts. Think of each social media platform as a different café, each with its own flavor. Facebook is great for all-round socializing, sharing news, and joining various interest groups. Instagram is perfect if you love photos and videos showing your garden blooms or culinary triumphs. Twitter? It's the place for quick updates, sharing thoughts, or keeping up with news. Set up an account by visiting the website or downloading the app and following the prompts. You'll need an email address or a phone number, and you'll create a password. Remember, making a strong password is like locking your front door—it keeps your account secure.

Managing privacy settings is crucial. These settings are like the curtains in your home; they control who sees what's inside. On Facebook, you can adjust who sees your posts or who can send you friend requests. Instagram lets you make your account private, meaning only people you approve can see your posts. Twitter gives you options to protect your tweets. Spend time exploring these settings to ensure your sharing is as public or private as possible. If in doubt, use the platform's help section for step-by-step guides or ask a family member or friend for assistance.

Now, onto the fun part—sharing and communicating. Want to share a photo? Click the plus sign on Instagram, select the photo from your gallery, add a fun caption or a few hashtags (those little phrases starting with a #), and share. It's like sending a postcard to everyone at once. Facebook allows more than just photos; you can write posts, share news articles, or even post a video. And when it comes to communicating, don't just scroll silently. Leave comments, click "like," or start a conversation. It's like chatting over the garden fence but in the digital world.

Joining groups and forums can be a delightful way to deepen your connections and find communities with similar interests. Are you a budding gardener? There's a group for that. Love knitting? There's a group for that, too. On Facebook, use the search bar to find groups by keywords. Once you find a group that interests you, join it to interact with members, share tips, and ask questions. It's like joining a club, but you don't have to leave your comfy chair.

Finally, let's talk about staying safe online because the internet, much like the real world, has its share of shady alleys. Be cautious with personal information. Sharing your full birthdate, address, or financial information can make you a scam target. Think twice before clicking on links, especially if they promise something sensational. Scammers often use such tactics to lure people into revealing personal information. They often create a sense of urgency to prompt quick action. If an offer or message seems suspicious, it probably is. When in doubt, double-check with someone you trust or look it up using a reliable source. Remember, staying safe online is just as important as enjoying the connectivity it brings.

So, there you have it, your primer for staying connected with family and friends through social media. With these tools at your fingertips, you're ready to explore the bustling, vibrant world of digital socializing. Share a photo, write a post, join a discussion, and keep those digital conversations flowing. Engage with others by responding to comments and asking open-ended questions to encourage interaction. Or you can also consider sharing relevant articles or resources to provide value and to spark up further discussions. It's a beautiful way to stay engaged, informed, and connected, bringing the global village right to your doorstep.

Hosting Events: Planning Small Gatherings

Think of your home as your private venue, where each gathering is a show you produce, direct, and star in! Planning small get-togethers can turn your home into a cozy place that is filled with laughter and fun talks. It's a great chance to make new friends and create happy memories. Sharing stories over good food and enjoying each other's company. These special moments can really brighten our lives. Let's walk through the cozy path of turning your next get-together into a warm, unforgettable event.

Firstly, the nuts and bolts of event planning start with crafting those charming invitations. In the digital age, an e-invite can be both a practical and a delightful way to announce your event. Websites like Evite or Paperless Post offer various customizable options that add a personal touch to every invite. However, suppose you're feeling a bit traditional or your gathering is intimate. In that case, a handmade card can add a unique, personal touch that shows your guests how much you care. Whichever method you choose, ensure your invitations clearly state the essentials: the who, what, when, and where of your event. Consider adding RSVP details to help you plan better. In this way, you can make sure everything runs smoothly and everyone is on the same page. Adding a personal note about why you're hosting the gathering can set a warm, welcoming tone from the start.

Setting up the space is where your inner decorator can shine. The key here is comfort meets style. Arrange your seating to encourage conversation; a circle or semicircle works best. Dim the lighting to create a cozy environment. Fairy lights or candles can quickly change the vibe of a room. And let's not forget the power of a well-curated playlist to set the mood. Music can be a conversation starter, a mood lifter, or a soothing background note to the evening's chatter.

Now, onto the fun part: choosing themes and activities to keep your guests engaged and entertained. Themes can range from a simple color theme, guiding your decorations and dress code, to more elaborate ones, like a retro night or a garden party. Activities should cater to the theme and the interests of your group, for instance, a wine tasting for a vineyard-themed party or board games for a game night. Consider adding music that fits the theme to light up the atmosphere. Also, you can think about including interactive activities, like DIY stations, to keep everyone engaged. Just remember, the idea is to create enjoyable and memorable experiences, giving your guests a night out and an unforgettable experience.

Hospitality is the heart of a good host. It's about creating an environment where everyone feels welcome and cared for. It starts with understanding your guests' preferences and needs. Are there dietary restrictions to consider? Any allergies? Ensure there's something on the menu for everyone. Small gestures, like personalized place cards or a parting gift, can make guests feel especially valued. Just be sure to stay attentive during the event! Think of yourself as both the host and a friendly guardian angel. Keep those drinks topped up, introduce your guests to each other, and make sure everyone's having a great time!

Utilizing gatherings to strengthen bonds is the most rewarding aspect of hosting. Regular get-togethers can transform acquaintances into close friends and deepen existing relationships. They create a tradition, a recurring joy that your friends and family can look forward to. Over time, these gatherings can become a cherished part of your social circle's rhythm, a safe space where everyone can relax, catch up, and make new memories together. They also provide an opportunity to celebrate milestones and achievements, strengthening the bonds among friends. Whether celebrating milestones, recuperating from a tough week, or enjoying good company, your gatherings can be a cornerstone of your social life, weaving a tapestry of relationships that enrich every aspect of your life.

So, why not start planning your next small gathering? Whether it's a sophisticated soiree or a casual catch-up, every event you host is an opportunity to create joy, foster connections, and show the people in your life how much they mean to you. Set the date, send out those invites, and let the magic of good company fill your home with warmth and laughter. After all, isn't life just a series of moments spent with others? Make each one count.

Bridge and Other Card Games: Learning to Play

Imagine a cozy evening, a table set with a deck of cards, and a room filled with the gentle buzz of friendly competition. Whether it's Bridge, Rummy, or Euchre, card games are not just about shuffling and dealing; they blend strategy, skill, and social interaction. Let's shuffle through the basics of these popular games, setting you up for many enjoyable game nights ahead.

Learning the basics of card games like Bridge or Rummy might initially seem daunting, but once you grasp the core principles, it's as easy as pie. Take Bridge, for example, a game of partnership where communication and strategy intertwine beautifully. The game begins with a bidding process, where you and your partner signal each other the strength of your hands and propose a contract on how many tricks you think you can win. It's an important time to communicate and strategize, as your bids will set the tone for the entire game.

The play then involves trying to win enough tricks to meet your contract, with each card played prompting mental gymnastics as you try to outwit your opponents. Similarly, Rummy is all about making sets and runs from the cards you're dealt, a perfect blend of luck and strategy as you decide which cards to keep and which to discard. With its brisk pace and emphasis on trump cards, Euchre offers yet another flavor of strategic thinking. Each game has its own set of rules and strategies that you can learn through online tutorials or books. You can also join a local club where experienced players can guide you along the way.

Organizing game nights is a fantastic way to turn your newfound card game skills into an evening filled with laughter and camaraderie. Start by gathering a group of friends or neighbors who share your interest in card games. Setting up is simple: a quiet room with a table large enough to accommodate your group, adequate lighting, and enough chairs. A few decks of cards and a scorepad for games that require scoring should complete your setup. Make the atmosphere welcoming with light snacks and beverages; think of easy finger foods and refreshing drinks. To keep the games lively and fun, why not switch up the card games every time you meet? You could even host mini-tournaments where the winner gets a little prize. It adds some friendly competition and excitement. Plus, it's a great way to keep everyone on their toes and having a blast. This keeps the competitive spirit alive and ensures your game nights stay fresh.

The social benefits of playing card games are immense. These games inherently require communication and interaction, which naturally fosters social connections. Each game becomes a mini-adventure as players navigate the rules, strategize together, and engage in light-hearted banter. For seniors, these game nights can be a lifeline to staying mentally agile and socially active. The mental stimulation in strategizing and remembering card suits and runs can improve cognitive functions. At the same time, social interaction helps ward off feelings of loneliness and isolation. It's a win-win, with the added bonus of a few laughs and the thrill of competition.

Expanding your social circle through card games is easier. Why not teach others as you become more confident in your card-playing skills? Sharing your knowledge of card games can be a wonderful way to meet new people and strengthen existing relationships. Organize a "learn to play" evening where you introduce others to your favorite card games. This gives you a chance to showcase your skills and helps you connect with others who share your interests. It's about passing on the joy of card games, one hand at a time.

Card games are more than just pastimes; they are gateways to enriched social interaction, mental exercise, and, quite simply, a great deal of fun. Whether holding a royal flush in a game of Bridge or laying down your final card in Rummy, each game you play weaves deeper social ties and brings joy and competition to your everyday life. So, deal the cards, place your bids, and let the games begin!

As this chapter on social connections wraps up, it's clear that the activities discussed here—from volunteering and joining clubs to playing card games—are not just ways to pass the time. They are meaningful engagements that enhance your social network, keep your mind active, and enrich your life with joy and purpose. As we dive into this next segment, just remember that every connection you make, every new hobby you try, and all those games you play add so much color to your retired life. It's all about enjoying those moments and creating wonderful experiences along the way. !Let's continue exploring and growing our social life by traveling on a budget to places near and far.

Chapter 6: Thriving on a Budget

Ah, retirement! It's like being handed a free pass to the amusement park—so many rides and attractions, yet the dilemma of where to spend your precious tokens so you can have the most fun without running out never leaves you! Thriving on a budget in retirement doesn't mean skimping on the joys of life; instead, it's about smart spending, finding those hidden gems that don't cost the earth but enrich your life immensely. So, let's roll up our sleeves and dive into the art of luxurious frugality, starting with one of the most exhilarating parts of retirement—travel!

Budget-Friendly Travel Destinations

Exploring Less Known Locations

Who says you must burn a hole in your pocket visiting the Eiffel Tower or the Statue of Liberty? Some of the most enchanting spots are the less trumpeted ones, hidden away from the tourist throngs, waiting to be discovered by a savvy traveler like you. These lesser-known destinations are not just kinder to your wallet but often offer a richer, more authentic experience. Think quaint villages, untouched beaches, and local festivals brimming with culture and charm that the glossy travel brochures often overlook. These hidden gems offer authentic experiences that allow you to connect with the heart and soul of a place in a way that popular destinations can't. From the wild, windswept coasts of Nova Scotia to the sun-soaked vineyards of rural Bulgaria, stepping off the beaten path can lead you to some spectacular spots that feel like they've been kept secret just for you. The thrill of discovery and the sense of adventure are yours to claim.

Utilizing Budget Travel Apps and Websites

Welcome to the golden age of travel, where technology is your trusted ally. With many travel apps and websites at your fingertips, finding the best deals on accommodation, flights, and local attractions has never been easier. Apps like Skyscanner and Hopper empower you to book flights at the lowest prices and advise on the best times to purchase tickets. Websites like Airbnb or Booking.com offer a range of lodging options, from cozy apartments to charming B&Bs, often at a fraction of the cost of hotels. And let's not forget about local deal websites like Groupon, where you can snag discounts on everything from guided tours to gourmet meals. Just a bit of time spent browsing these resources can really pay off! It puts you in control of your travel plans and makes luxury travel way more affordable. You'll be surprised at how much you can save and still enjoy an amazing getaway!

Traveling During Off-Peak Seasons

Traveling during off-peak times can be a game-changer if you're not bound by the school calendar or peak holiday seasons. Not only are flights and accommodations cheaper, but you'll also enjoy destinations without the crush of peak-season crowds. Imagine strolling through the streets of Venice in early spring or exploring the ancient temples of Cambodia during the fall. The weather is still lovely, and with fewer tourists around, you have a great chance to really dive into the local lifestyle. It's the perfect time to soak it all in! Plus, many attractions offer lower prices during these times, so you can see more without spending more.

Benefiting From Senior Discounts

One of the perks of reaching the golden years is the plethora of discounts available to you, and travel is no exception. Many airlines, hotels, and attractions offer significant senior discounts that can make a big difference to your travel budget. These discounts are not just about saving money; they are a token of appreciation for your years of hard work and a sign of respect for your life experience. They also encourage you to explore new opportunities and enjoy well-deserved perks! Please don't be shy about asking for these discounts; sometimes, they're not advertised. From reduced fares on public transport in Europe to discounted entry fees at national parks and museums worldwide, these savings add up, allowing you to splurge on a fancy dinner or a unique souvenir. Remember to carry any ID or documentation that proves your age, and watch your travel costs drop as your adventures soar.

Traveling on a budget doesn't mean compromising on the quality of your experiences. It's all about being resourceful and taking advantage of the many options out there that can save you money while making your travel adventures even better! So, pack your bags, grab your sense of adventure, and prepare to explore the world without draining your wallet. The road less traveled is waiting, and it's surprisingly affordable!

Eating Well on a Fixed Income: Healthy and Cheap Recipes

Whoever said that eating well on a dime was impossible must not have had the pleasure of savoring a hearty stew made from seasonal veggies or the joy of snipping fresh herbs right from their own garden! Let's bust some myths and explore the fun of cooking up tasty, healthy meals that are easy on the wallet! You'll see that you don't have to sacrifice flavor for savings! With a pinch of planning and some creativity, your kitchen can become the source of delicious and economical meals.

Smart Grocery Shopping

Shopping smart is the first step towards maintaining a budget-friendly kitchen. Begin by embracing the world of coupons and weekly deals. Local newspapers, store flyers, and online platforms can be gold mines for discounts. Apps like Honey or Flipp digitally gather coupons for you, making it easier to save without the hassle of clipping physical coupons. Next, consider buying in bulk. Items like rice, beans, pasta, and even certain spices are often cheaper in larger quantities. Plus, it cuts down on packaging waste and means you won't run out of your favorites anytime soon! Just ensure you have enough storage space to keep everything fresh and organized. Another savvy shopping strategy is focusing on seasonal produce. Vegetables and fruits are less expensive when in season and at their peak flavor and nutritional value. Plan your meals around what's currently abundant. For instance, think zucchini and berries in the summer or squash and apples in the fall. This approach saves money and adds a delightful seasonal freshness to your meals.

Cooking Nutritious and Low-Cost Meals

Now, let's use those innovative shopping strategies with simple, cost-effective recipes. A great start is a classic vegetable stir-fry. Use whatever veggies you've found on sale or grown yourself, toss them with some soy sauce and a splash of sesame oil, and serve over a bed of rice. Not only is this meal quick and easy, but it also uses inexpensive and nourishing ingredients. Another budget-friendly favorite is lentil soup. Lentils are a powerhouse of nutrition, rich in proteins and fiber, and incredibly cheap. Simmer them with diced tomatoes, carrots, onions, and a few herbs for a satisfying dish that tastes even better as leftovers. Don't underestimate the power of the humble egg! It's packed with protein and super versatile, perfect for everything from veggie-loaded frittatas to a classic egg salad sandwich. You can't go wrong with it!

Meal Planning and Preparation

One of the most effective ways to stretch your food budget is through meal planning. Start by taking inventory of what you already have in your pantry and fridge. Then, plan your weekly meals around these ingredients, adding only the necessary items to your shopping list. This method saves money and also reduces food waste. Prep meals in advance to save time and ensure you always have a healthy option. For instance, you can cook a large batch of chili and freeze it in portions or prepare salad jars ready to grab-and-go. Remember, a little time spent planning and prepping can lead to substantial savings and less stress during meal times.

Growing Your Own Herbs and Vegetables

Finally, consider cultivating a small garden. It's a beautiful way to have fresh produce at your fingertips and can significantly cut your grocery bills. Start with easy-to-grow herbs like basil, cilantro, or mint. Expand to vegetables like tomatoes, peppers, or greens if you have space. Homegrown veggies are fresher and tastier, and gardening itself is a relaxing and rewarding hobby. Cooking with ingredients you've raised yourself is heartwarming, adding an extra sprinkle of joy to every dish.

Embracing these strategies can transform the way you shop, cook, and enjoy food. It's about making thoughtful choices that maximize your budget without compromising nutrition or flavor. So, here's to delicious meals that keep your belly and wallet full!

Free Entertainment Resources for Seniors

Who said the best things in life cost a fortune? When it comes to entertainment and learning, there's a treasure trove of free goodies just waiting to be explored, especially for savvy seniors looking to expand their horizons without stretching their wallets. Let's start with a classic cornerstone of community resources: your local library. Libraries are not just about books; they are cultural hubs offering a variety of free activities and resources that might surprise you. Libraries are amazing for so many reasons! You can borrow the latest bestsellers and e-books, plus they often host workshops and lecture series on all kinds of topics. It's a great way to stay intellectually engaged and keep your mind buzzing! Many libraries also offer free access to computers and the internet, as well as subscriptions to digital magazines, academic journals, and even streaming services like Kanopy, which provides a variety of free films and documentaries. Check out your local library's calendar for events; you might find book clubs, craft workshops, or even free tech tutoring sessions—perfect for mastering that new tablet or smartphone!

Now, let's step out into the community. Many local parks, community centers, and universities host free events that can turn an ordinary day into an adventure. Summer concerts in the park, art exhibitions at local galleries, outdoor movie nights, and community festivals are just a few examples of how you can entertain yourself without spending a dime. Make sure to check out community bulletin boards and local newspapers, or swing by town websites to keep up with all the upcoming events. It's a great way to stay in the loop and find fun things to do! These outings provide free entertainment and allow you to socialize and connect with fellow community members. It's a beautiful way to experience new forms of entertainment and culture right in your backyard.

If we turn to the digital world, the internet is a goldmine of free entertainment options tailored to various interests. For film buffs, websites like Pluto TV or Classic Cinema Online offer an array of free movies, from golden age classics to modern indie films. If puzzles and games are more your style, sites like JigZone and Pogo host free puzzles and games that can help keep your mind sharp while providing hours of fun. Many educational platforms offer free webinars and lectures for those eager to learn. *TED Talks*, for instance, can be a fantastic source of inspiration and knowledge, covering topics from science to art. You can also often find online courses that let you dive even deeper into subjects that interest you!

You can watch these at your leisure, learning and growing from the comfort of your home.

Lastly, let's talk about volunteering. Volunteering isn't just a noble way to give back to the community; it's also a great source of free social interaction and learning. Whether helping out at a local theater, assisting in community gardens, or participating in events at the local museum, volunteering allows you to connect with like-minded individuals, learn new skills, and even stay physically active. Many organizations truly appreciate the wisdom and experience seniors offer. In return, volunteering can give you a refreshing sense of purpose and help you feel more connected to your community! Volunteering in cultural or community centers can usually grant you free access to events and activities you might otherwise pay for.

By taking advantage of these free resources, you're not only enriching your lifestyle but also building connections in your community. It just goes to show that staying actively engaged can be fun and affordable! So, go ahead and take full advantage of these opportunities. After all, the best things in life really are free, especially when they bring learning, joy, and a sense of community fitting to your doorstep.

DIY Home Decor: Affordable Crafting

The joy of transforming the old into something new and beautiful! DIY home decor isn't just about saving money; it's about infusing your personal touch into your living space, making it uniquely yours. It's like being an artist, except your canvas is your home, and your paints are bits and bobs you find around the house or pick up from a thrift store. Let's roll up our sleeves and dive into the world of affordable crafting, where creativity meets frugality in a delightful dance.

Repurposing Old Items

Do you know those glass jars you've been saving? Do you think they might come in handy one day? Well, their time to shine is now! Turning old jars into chic vases is as simple as giving them a coat of paint or wrapping them in twine or fabric. Imagine a row of these, each filled with fresh flowers or LED lights, lining your windowsill or gracing your dining table. And don't stop at jars. Is that old ladder languishing in the garage? Sand it down, give it a fresh lick of paint, and use it as a quirky bookshelf or a towel rack. Old furniture can also get a new lease on life with just a bit of creativity. A dresser, for instance, can be transformed into a stunning kitchen island with some paint and new handles, adding character and functionality to your kitchen.

Using Affordable Crafting Supplies

Crafting doesn't have to be an expensive hobby. With some savvy shopping, you can find crafting supplies that won't break the bank. Start by visiting local thrift stores and yard sales, where you can find everything from fabrics and yarn to old frames and furniture that can be upcycled. Online marketplaces like eBay or Facebook Marketplace are also treasure troves for affordable crafting materials. Be sure to keep an eye out for sales at local craft stores as well. Often, you can buy remnants of fabrics, offcuts of wood, and other materials at a fraction of the cost. Just keep an eye out for items that might not seem like much at first, but with a bit of creativity and some hard work, you can really transform them!

Simple DIY Projects

Ready to start crafting? Here are a couple of simple projects that anyone can tackle. First, consider creating your own wall art. It can be as simple as framing a beautiful piece of fabric or a page from an old illustrated book. Or, take it a step further by painting a simple mural directly onto a wall or a canvas. Use painter's tape to create geometric shapes or stripes, then fill in with colors that match your decor. Another project could be making your own throw pillows. Find some vintage fabric or repurpose old clothes, sew them into covers, and stuff them with filling. Not only is this project cost-effective, but it also adds a splash of color and comfort to your living room or bedroom.

Organizing Crafting Sessions

Crafting is more fun with company! Why not organize a crafting session with friends or community members? It's a great way to socialize and share skills, and you can even swap supplies, ensuring everyone has something new to work with without spending a dime. Choose a project everyone can enjoy, whether it's making holiday decorations, custom tote bags, or even simple jewelry. Set up a space where everyone has room to work, perhaps with a central table for shared supplies. Play some music, serve some snacks, and enjoy the camaraderie that comes from creating something together. Not only do you walk away with a lovely item for your home, but you also create lasting memories with friends and neighbors.

Diving into DIY home decor projects is like opening a box of chocolates; you never know what you'll get, but it's sure to be delightful. With a bit of creativity and some basic supplies, you can really bring new life to older items. It's all about seeing the potential in what you already have. This way, you can turn your living space into a reflection of your personality and style, all while keeping your budget in check! So, grab those crafting tools and let your creativity flow, turning your home into a gallery of your own making.

Low-Cost Fitness Options

Who said staying fit has to wrestle your wallet to the ground? Not in your golden years, not ever! Fitness is a treasure that should be accessible without having to splash the cash. Let's lace up those sneakers (or comfy walking shoes) and explore some fantastic, budget-friendly ways to keep that spring in your step. Whether it's the charm of a leafy park trail or the convenience of a living room yoga session, staying active doesn't have to cost a dime.

Walking and Jogging Paths

There's a whole world out there ready to be your gym, and it's right outside your door. With their sprawling walking paths and scenic jogging trails, local parks are a gold mine for anyone looking to boost their fitness without spending a penny. These community gems offer more than just a track; they provide a refreshing environment to soak in the beauty of nature and listen to the birds. You can even do some people-watching while getting your heart rate up! Engaging with your surroundings makes the exercise feel less like a chore and more like a leisurely pastime. Regular walks or jogs in these natural settings can significantly improve your cardiovascular health, mood, and overall energy levels. These activities are incredibly flexible; you can set your own pace and gradually increase the intensity as your fitness improves. So, grab a friend or enjoy some quality "me time;" either way, you're making strides towards better health.

Community Center Fitness Classes

Your local community center is likely a hub of activity, and it's worth taking a closer look at what they offer in terms of fitness classes. Many centers provide a range of options from aerobics to Zumba, often at a fraction of the cost you'd expect. These classes are typically designed to cater to all levels, including beginners and seniors, ensuring everyone can participate safely and effectively. One of the best things about taking a class at your community center is that you get a great workout while also building a sense of community! It's a win-win! It's a chance to meet neighbors, make new friends, and even find workout buddies who can keep you motivated.

Additionally, these centers often have seasonal promotions or loyalty discounts, making it even more affordable to stay active. It's worth calling them or checking their website to see what's available. Remember, every step towards fitness is a step towards a more vibrant, energetic you.

Home-Based Exercise Routines

Now, let's talk about the convenience of home workouts. With the abundance of online resources available today, you can set up an effective exercise routine right in your living room. From YouTube fitness channels to various fitness apps, you can find guided workouts that require minimal to no equipment. Plus, many of these resources are totally free! Focus on routines that enhance flexibility, strength, and cardiovascular health, key areas that contribute to a well-rounded fitness regime. For instance, chair exercises are fantastic for flexibility and can be done while watching your favorite morning show. For strength, you might try body-weight exercises like squats, wall push-ups, or even simple weight lifting using household items like water bottles. Remember, the goal is to keep your body moving, so even a few minutes of structured exercise can make a big difference.

Yoga and Meditation Apps

Let's not overlook the wonders of yoga and meditation in the spirit of keeping both body and mind limber. Several apps offer free or inexpensive yoga routines, which can be a fantastic addition to your daily schedule. Apps like Daily Yoga offer a variety of sessions aimed at improving flexibility, balance, and strength, all of which are vital as we age. Meditation apps like Insight Timer or Headspace provide guided meditation, which can help reduce stress and improve mental clarity. Incorporating these practices into your daily routine can enhance your physical health and bring a profound sense of calm and focus to your day. It's all about finding the perfect balance!

Embracing these low-cost fitness options opens up a world of possibilities for maintaining your health and vitality. Whether exploring the great outdoors, joining a class, or rolling out a yoga mat in your living room, each activity brings you one step closer to a healthier, happier you. So, why not start today? Your body (and your wallet) will thank you!

Thrifting: Finding Gems in Second-Hand Shopping

Thrifting is like a treasure hunt where you're not just saving money; you're rescuing relics and giving them a second chance at life. Whether it's a vintage lamp that reminds you of your grandmother's house or a classic leather jacket straight out of a 90's sitcom, thrifting is all about the thrill of the find. But effective thrifting is more than luck; it's an art form. Let's dive into mastering this art, turning old items into new treasures without breaking the bank.

Thrifting can be wildly successful with a few insider tips. First, timing is everything. Regular visits can increase your chances of finding great items because stock changes frequently. Shopping early in the morning or on weekdays is usually the way to go! The stores are less crowded, so you can take your time browsing without feeling rushed. Knowing what to look for is crucial, too. Focus on items that are not only visually appealing but also of good quality. Check for signs of wear and tear, but remember, a little scratch or a missing button can often be fixed. Knowing the market value of items is also helpful, especially if you're looking for collectibles or antiques. This way, you can spot a deal when you see one.

The benefits of second-hand shopping stretch beyond the wallet. Environmentally, it's a win-win. By purchasing used items, you're helping reduce waste and the demand for new resources. Plus, you can often find unique pieces that add character to your home! Economically, it allows you to stretch your dollars further, getting more for less. This is particularly beneficial for those on a fixed income, as it enables a lifestyle that includes variety and quality without the accompanying price tag. Each unique find adds character and story to your life, making your purchases all the more special.

Restyling found items is where your creativity really gets to shine. That old dresser? A fresh coat of paint and new knobs can transform it into an elegant piece for your bedroom or a quirky bookshelf for the living room. An old ladder can become a charming vertical garden for your herbs, adding both functionality and style to your patio. It's also a great way to maximize space and make your outdoor area feel more vibrant! The possibilities are endless, and often, the only limit is your imagination. Online tutorials and DIY blogs can be great sources of inspiration and instruction, helping you turn your vision into reality.

Organizing a thrifting excursion with friends or community members can amplify the fun. Not only does it make the hunt more enjoyable, but it also provides a platform for sharing tips and ideas. You might organize a theme for each outing, and perhaps one trip focused on finding the best vintage clothing, another on locating perfect home decor items. Sharing the experience can lead to shared joy, especially when someone finds that perfect item they've been seeking. It's like a collective celebration of each other's thrifting victories. Also, swapping stories about your finds can make the hunt even more fun and inspiring!

Thrifting isn't just shopping; it's an adventure that saves you money, sparks your creativity, and contributes to a more sustainable planet. It's about seeing the potential in the forgotten and the flair in the old. So, dust off that old hat, grab a shopping bag, and step into the world of thrift shopping. Who knows what treasures await?

As we wrap up this chapter on thriving on a budget, remember that it's all about making the most of what you have and finding joy in the unexpected. Whether through travel, cooking, entertainment, or shopping, there are endless opportunities to enrich your life without emptying your wallet. Thrifting is just one piece of the puzzle, offering a way to embrace sustainability, unleash creativity, and enjoy the thrill of the hunt, all while keeping an eye on economics. As we move on to the next chapter, let's carry forward this spirit of resourcefulness and adventure, exploring even more ways to enrich our lives in retirement through creative arts such as painting, drawing, poetry, and languages.

Chapter 7: Cultivating Creativity and Learning

Think of retirement as your personal renaissance, a time ripe for exploration and expression in the vibrant world of art. If you've ever dreamed of painting a sunset that rivals Van Gogh's strokes or sketching the serene beauty of your garden, now is the perfect moment to dip your brushes into the colorful world of painting and drawing. Creating art is about expressing your inner self. It allows you to find peace in the solitude of your own creative space. You might even surprise yourself with what you can bring to life on canvas or paper.

Painting and Drawing: Starting with the Basics

Choosing Your Tools

Start this artistic journey by selecting the right tools. Think of an artist's tools as an extension of their vision—what you choose can shape the path of your creations. For those just starting out, exploring different brushes, paints, and papers might seem as complex as deciding what to watch on Netflix on a Friday night, but worry not! Let's simplify the process.

First, let's talk about brushes. A few basic brushes will serve most of your needs. A flat brush is perfect for bold, sweeping strokes, while a small round brush can define those intricate details that bring a painting to life. As for paint, watercolors are wonderfully forgiving for beginners, offering the ability to blend beautiful washes of color. Acrylics are a great choice, too; they're versatile, fast-drying, and can mimic the properties of oil and watercolor paints, depending on how you use them.

Don't forget the canvas! Starting with paper is less intimidating; opt for thick, quality paper that won't buckle under the weight of your artistic endeavors. As you get more confident, go ahead and try out canvases or wood panels. It'll add a cool new dimension to your art. Remember, the best tools are the ones that feel right in your hands and suit the visions in your mind.

Fundamental Techniques

Now, let's break down some basic techniques and make them easy to understand. Every great masterpiece starts with a simple sketch. Grab your pencil and lightly sketch your vision before committing to paint. This rough outline will guide your hand and help prevent any "Oh, I didn't mean to paint that there" moments.

Next up is color mixing—don't worry, you won't need a chemistry degree for this. Start with your primary colors: red, yellow, and blue; experiment by mixing them to discover the wide range of colors you can create. Want a stunning shade of green? Mix blue and yellow. Dreaming of a vibrant purple? Red and blue are your friends. Play around, and don't be afraid to make mud; every artist does it at some point.

Let's not forget about brushwork. The way you use your brush can greatly change the mood of your painting. Long, fluid strokes can convey calmness and tranquility, while short, sharp strokes might express dynamic energy or tension. Practice different brush techniques on scrap paper; see how the brush moves and the paint responds.

Setting Up a Creative Space

Creating a dedicated space for your art sets the stage for productivity. It signals your brain that it's time to switch to creative mode. This space doesn't need to be an expansive studio; an inviting corner of your living room or a quiet spot by the window can work just fine. Ensure good lighting; natural light is best, but a well-placed lamp can also do wonders. Keep your tools organized and within easy reach; a tidy space is inviting and less distracting. Make your space feel personal by adding things that inspire you, like photos of your favorite places or artwork from artists you love. Make this space your own—an artistic sanctuary where creativity flows freely.

Finding Inspiration

Inspiration ignites creativity and can be found all around you, from the vastness of the ocean to the delicate patterns of leaves on a tree in your backyard. Take a nature walk, camera in hand, and capture whatever catches your eye. Visit local art galleries or browse online museums (Google Arts & Culture offers a virtual treasure trove of artwork from around the world) to learn from the masters. Read poetry, watch a dramatic sunset, or people-watch at a café. Inspiration is endless; it's all about keeping your senses open and receptive to the world around you.

Exploring painting and drawing can be one of the most rewarding and fulfilling experiences during your retirement. It's a journey of artistic skill, personal discovery, and expression. So why not grab that brush or pencil? Your canvas awaits, and who knows what beautiful creations are waiting to be brought to life by your hand? Let the colors flow, the lines wander, and your spirit soar on the wings of your newfound artistic freedom.

Writing Poetry: Expressing Feelings with Words

Imagine transforming your whirlwind of emotions into a symphony of words that dance gracefully across a page. With its rhythmic beats and resonant verses, poetry offers a profound way to express what's in your heart and mind. Whether you're watching a sunset that paints the sky in hues of gold and purple, reminiscing about first love, or simply enjoying the quiet moments of your morning coffee, poetry turns these slices of life into artful narratives. Let's explore the different types of poetry and how you can use it to express your feelings and experiences.

Poetry comes in a delightful array of styles, each with its own rules and liberties. If you like structure, a sonnet might be for you. Its 14 lines and specific rhyme scheme are great for expressing love, sadness, or deep thoughts. On the other hand, haikus, with their three-line briefness focused on nature and emotion, can capture a moment with a sharpness that rivals the clarity of a photograph. Then there's free verse, which breaks free from the traditional constraints of meter and rhyme, offering you the freedom to write as you think in a stream of consciousness that can be both liberating and evocative.

Diving into poetry begins with understanding and employing fundamental literary techniques that act as the tools of the trade. Metaphors and similes enhance your poems by creating comparisons that spark strong images or feelings. For example, you could describe a tough time in your life as a "storm that washed over my spirit," using the metaphor to show how deeply it affected you. Similarly, a simile could paint a picture of your calm demeanor as "cool as a lake on a windless day," providing a visual anchor that deepens the reader's emotional understanding of your words.

Imagery is another cornerstone of poetic beauty, creating a sensory experience for the reader. To master this, focus on incorporating visual, auditory, or tactile details that bring your scenes to life. Describe not just the sight of autumn leaves but the sound of them crunching underfoot, the smell of rain on the damp earth, and the calm whisper of wind accompanying the changing seasons. These details turn your poetry from simple sentences into a vivid, engaging experience.

If you're eager to refine your craft and share your work, consider joining a poetry writing workshop. These workshops can be fantastic incubators for your artistry, providing a space to receive constructive feedback and engage with fellow poets who can offer new perspectives on your work. Local community centers, libraries, and even online platforms host sessions that can fit into your schedule. These gatherings polish your poems and build a community of like-minded individuals who share your passion for poetry.

Once you have a collection of poems, you feel the pull to share them with a broader audience. Publishing your poetry can be as simple as submitting to community newsletters or as ambitious as creating a blog to publish your work online. Platforms like WordPress and Medium allow you to reach readers across the globe, turning your personal reflections into public art. If you dream of having a book of your own poems, self-publishing is a great option. There are many services available to assist you, from creating manuscripts to printing books.

Engaging in poetry is like having a dialogue with your deepest self; it's about finding the essence of your emotions and experiences and translating them into words that resonate. Whether through the structured elegance of a sonnet or the unrestrained freedom of free verse, poetry offers a powerful way to understand and share your view of the world. So, why not grab a pen and let the rhythm of your thoughts guide you to create something extraordinary? Your next poem might be touching someone's heart or, perhaps, your own.

Learning a New Language: Tips and Resources

Imagine being able to order a croissant in flawless French on your next trip to Paris or sharing stories with your grandkids in Spanish during family dinners. Learning a new language isn't just about mastering grammar and vocabulary; it's about opening doors to new cultures, connecting more deeply with loved ones, or simply keeping your brain sharp and agile. The joy of learning a new language in retirement is that you can pick one that aligns with your travel dreams, family ties, or simply your passion for languages.

Selecting which language to dive into can be as exciting as planning a vacation. Start by considering your motivations: Are you itching to explore your ancestral roots, or perhaps you have a bucket list destination where a particular language dominates? If your grandchildren speak a second language, learning it also offers an excellent way to bond and communicate with them on a new level. Consider the cultural content you enjoy, films, music, or cuisine, as this can serve as both inspiration and a practical context to use the language. Once you've pinpointed your why, choosing your what becomes a delightful decision rather than a daunting dilemma.

Now, onto the how—integrating language learning into your daily routine can be seamless and enjoyable with the right strategies. One effective way to learn is to incorporate it into activities you already enjoy. Enjoy cooking? Try following recipes in the target language. Avid reader? Start with children's books in a new language, which are easier to understand and absorb. You can also label items around your home with their names in the language you're learning, turning every glance at the microwave or window into a mini-learning session.

Technology offers a rich repository of resources that make learning flexible and accessible. Language learning apps like Duolingo or Babbel are user-friendly. They can be customized to your pace and level, providing daily practice exercises that make learning a part of your routine. For a deeper learning experience, platforms like Rosetta Stone use images to help you think directly in the new language instead of translating it into English. These apps often include speech recognition technology to help you perfect your pronunciation—a handy feature when you're eager to chat up locals on your next trip abroad!

Finding and joining a community language class can add a valuable social element to your language-learning adventure. Many community colleges and adult education centers offer language courses that are both affordable and geared explicitly toward older adults, making the learning environment supportive and relatable. These classes offer the advantage of interacting directly with an instructor and classmates who are also learning, providing real-time feedback and opportunities for spontaneous conversation that you can't get from textbooks. Additionally, conversation groups, often found in libraries or community centers, provide informal settings where you can practice speaking and listening in a stress-free environment. These groups can be advantageous, as they build your confidence in speaking and understanding the language in a dynamic and interactive setting.

If you're tech-savvy or curious to become so, leveraging online resources can propel your language learning to new heights. Websites like iTalki or Tandem connect you with native speakers for practice via video or chat, giving you a taste of real-life conversations. For a more structured approach, online platforms such as Coursera or EdX offer language courses from universities worldwide, often for free or at a low cost. These courses can provide a comprehensive learning experience, complete with assignments, quizzes, and sometimes certificates that celebrate your progress.

Exploring a new language opens up a range of experiences and opportunities that enhance your life, making each day more exciting. Whether you're decoding the lyrics of French chanson, ordering tapas in Spanish, or simply enjoying a foreign film without subtitles, each little victory boosts your confidence and reminds you that learning, like life, is a delightful adventure that doesn't stop at retirement. So why not choose a language today and start blending new words into your everyday life? Who knows, the next conversation you strike up in another language might lead to a friendship or insight that could change your perspective in beautiful ways.

DIY Projects: Creating Useful Items for Home

Roll up your sleeves and clear some space on your workbench or kitchen table because we're diving into the gratifying world of Do-It-Yourself (DIY) projects! There's something profoundly satisfying about turning a pile of materials into a functional object with your hands. DIY projects fuel your creativity and add a personal touch to your home, whether it's a custom picture frame to hold memories of your grand adventures or a nifty shelf organizer to keep your spices in order.

Let's start with some simple projects that don't require you to transform your living room into a full-scale workshop. Picture frames, for instance, are a perfect first project. You can create a custom frame tailored to your desired size and style with bare wooden planks, a saw, and some glue. Imagine framing that painting you completed last month or a cherished photo of your family reunion. The personal satisfaction of looking at something beautiful that you framed yourself is unmatched. Similarly, building a shelf organizer can be as simple as repurposing old wooden boxes or crates. A bit of sanding, a dash of paint, some creative arrangement, and voila! You have an eco-friendly solution to your cluttered pantry or workshop.

Let's talk about tools and safety because even the simplest projects require some basic gear and precautions. Basic tools for most home projects include a hammer, screwdriver, measuring tape, and maybe a saw if you're comfortable making cuts. Investing in good quality tools can make a significant difference in the ease and enjoyment of your projects. Safety, of course, is the most important. Always wear protective eyewear when cutting or sanding; gloves can protect your hands from splinters and blisters. Keep your workspace tidy and tools organized to avoid any accidents. Remember, the goal is to enjoy and not rush through the process. Take your time to learn the proper use of each tool, and respect the power and potential of each gadget in your toolkit.

Upcycling is not just a trendy buzzword; it's a creative and environmentally friendly way to give old furniture or household items a new lease on life. Have an old ladder that's not safe for climbing? Turn it into a rustic bookshelf or a quirky plant stand. Or perhaps you've got a dresser that's seen better days? A little sandpaper, some paint, and new knobs can transform it into a chic credenza. Upcycling is like a puzzle; you look at what you have and imagine what it could become. It's about seeing beyond the surface wear and tear and envisioning the potential lurking beneath. This method saves money and reduces waste, making your DIY projects beneficial for both your home and the environment.

Lastly, why not share the joy of making with others? Organizing DIY sessions with family or community members can turn crafting into a social event that's both fun and fulfilling. Plan a "Make It Day" where everyone brings a small project or contributes to a communal one. These gatherings can be excellent opportunities to share skills, learn from each other, and enjoy the camaraderie of creating together. It's a great way to bond with grandchildren who can learn practical skills and the value of handmade items. Plus, it's a fantastic opportunity to pass on traditional crafts that might otherwise be lost to time. Whether building birdhouses or creating custom coasters, each project offers a chance to create objects, relationships, and memories.

Starting DIY projects is like opening a treasure chest of potential. Every raw material promises transformation, and every tool is a key to unlocking creativity. So, whether you're crafting solo or with loved ones, remember that each measure, cut, and nail is a step towards something beautiful—not just in what you create but in the experience itself.

Music Appreciation: Understanding Classical to Contemporary

Imagine yourself as a musical explorer, setting off on a delightful journey through the rich landscapes of sound that span centuries and cultures. From the difficult sounds of classical music to the smooth rhythms of jazz and the catchy beats of pop, music is a language that touches everyone's heart. But it's not just about listening; it's about understanding and appreciating the diversity of musical genres that make up the soundtrack of human history. Let's turn up the volume on our musical adventure and tune into the vast world of melodies, rhythms, and harmonies that await us.

Exploring different music genres is like sampling a buffet of the world's finest cuisines; each genre offers a unique flavor and a new perspective on sound. Start with classical music, the grand ancestor of many music styles. Dive into the works of Beethoven, Mozart, and Bach to experience the complexity and emotional depth of compositions that have stood the test of time. Next, dive into the world of jazz, where improvisation takes the lead, and every performance is a unique creation. Artists like Louis Armstrong and Ella Fitzgerald can introduce you to the spontaneity and expressive freedom of jazz, a genre that evolved from the heart of American culture.

Don't stop there; rock and roll with the energetic beats of the Beatles or the Rolling Stones, and see how rock music became the voice of a generation craving change. Then, enjoy the energetic bass lines of funk or let the moving lyrics of folk music carry you away, with each telling stories of life's challenges and successes. In today's music scene, pop artists like Taylor Swift and Bruno Mars blend multiple influences to create catchy tunes that dominate the airwaves. By exploring these genres, you broaden your musical horizons and deepen your appreciation for the artistry and cultural contexts that shape different musical styles.

Attending live performances can transform your appreciation of music from a passive listening experience to an electrifying and communal event. There's something magical about experiencing music in the moment, surrounded by fellow enthusiasts. Start by checking out the schedules of local theaters and concert halls, which often feature a variety of musical acts throughout the year. Community centers and universities also host live performances that can be both high-quality and affordable. Keep an eye out for music festivals in your area, too; they can be a fantastic way to experience a wide array of music styles over a few days. Going to these live events not only supports artists and enhances your cultural experiences but also connects you with a lively community of music fans.

A little homework can be incredibly enriching to truly appreciate the depth and breadth of any music genre. Delve into the history of the musical movements that pique your interest. Many community colleges and libraries offer courses or lectures on music history, giving you insights into how different styles evolved and the pioneers behind them. Numerous documentaries and books on music history are available for a more informal learning setup. These resources can help you connect the dots between different musical eras and understand the influences that shaped the sounds we love today.

Hosting listening parties is a fabulous way to share your passion for music while enjoying social interaction. Invite friends and family to a night of music exploration at your home. Pick a theme for each gathering, perhaps an evening of classical music masterpieces or a dive into the roots of rock and roll. Encourage guests to bring their favorite tracks related to the theme and spend the evening discussing the elements of music, sharing personal anecdotes related to the songs, and simply enjoying the company. These gatherings make music appreciation a shared joy and strengthen bonds with those around you through the universal language of music.

Exploring music appreciation fills your life with beautiful sounds and captivating stories. It's a journey that invites you to experience the past and present of music, deepening your understanding and enjoyment of this art form that plays such a vital role in human culture. So, tune your ears to the diverse melodies of the world, and let music be a source of joy, inspiration, and connection in your life.

Acting and Theater: Participating in Local Productions

Picture yourself in a world where you can be anyone from a Shakespearean hero to a modern-day detective, making new friends and igniting your creativity. Joining a local theater group can be your ticket to this exhilarating world. Whether you've always wanted to act or are just curious about theater, community theater is welcoming and includes people of all skill levels.

To get started, check out your local community centers or search online for theater groups near you. Many groups seek new members and are more than willing to guide novices. Don't worry about having a polished audition piece; the key here is enthusiasm and a willingness to learn. Once you're in, the spectrum of opportunities is broad. You might start with minor roles, a great way to dip your toes into acting without the pressure of carrying a major scene. Remember, every actor brings something unique to a role, no matter how small it might seem. Your role is important to the story's magic, as every line you deliver and every emotion you express adds depth to the entire production.

Understanding the basics of theater isn't just about learning lines. It involves mastering stage presence. The art of owning the space around you and connecting with the audience without uttering a single word. Practice projecting your voice to reach the back of the room without shouting. Learn to express emotions with your body language. Things like how you walk, hold your head, or move your hands can communicate just as much as your words. Plus, being aware of your body language can help you connect better with your audience and make your performance even more impactful. Local workshops or classes can be priceless in honing these skills. They provide a safe space to experiment and learn from more experienced actors and are a lot of fun, too!

But what if being in the spotlight isn't quite your thing? There's so much more to theater than what happens on stage. Participating behind the scenes can be just as rewarding and creatively satisfying. Every production requires a strong backstage team to manage tasks like set design, costume creation, and lighting and sound. These roles are perfect for those who love to create and organize but prefer to stay out of the limelight. Volunteering to help with set construction or painting can be a great way to be involved. You'll learn about the creative process that brings a physical environment to life, contributing to the atmosphere and realism of the performance while also developing teamwork skills that are essential in any production.

The benefits of getting involved in theater are manifold. Socially, you'll meet a diverse group of passionate individuals who share your interest in the arts. The friendship in a theater group is really strong; rehearsals and performances help everyone connect as they work together toward a shared goal. Plus, it's a great way to meet new people and build lasting memories along the way! Cognitively, memorizing lines and cues can sharpen your memory and improve concentration. Acting lets you express feelings you might not usually share, giving you a chance to release those emotions. It can also help you gain a better understanding of yourself and others, making it a really rewarding experience. The joy of performance, the applause, and the shared success of a production can significantly boost your self-confidence and overall happiness.

Joining a theater group offers more than just an activity; it provides a dynamic, supportive community where creativity thrives. Whether you're center stage or behind the curtains, you play a pivotal role in the magical world of theater. So why not take the leap? The applause at the end of a great show isn't just for the performance; it's also for you, celebrating your bravery in trying something new. It's a chance to feel proud of your hard work and the connections you've made along the way.

Reflecting on Theater's Role in Personal Growth

Theater is more than an art form; it's a transformative experience that enriches your life. It challenges you to learn new skills, step into different characters, and see the world from varied perspectives. Each role is a new adventure, and each performance is an opportunity to touch your audience's and fellow cast members' hearts. The lessons you learn here go beyond the stage; they can really improve your personal interactions and boost your empathy and understanding. Plus, they can help you communicate better and connect with others on a deeper level.

As we wrap up this discussion on building creativity and learning, keep in mind that the arts are a fantastic way to connect with others and discover new sides of yourself. Whether through painting, writing, language, or theater, each creative pursuit offers a path to personal fulfillment and joy. So, embrace your creative passions and let them lead you to new adventures and friendships. As we move on to the next chapter, let's hold onto the excitement of exploration and the joy of discovery that modern technology and the digital age bring. Using these tools can help us learn more and connect with even more people along the way.

Chapter 8: Embracing the Digital Age

Ah, the digital age! It's like being at a perpetual high school reunion. Everyone you've ever known is just a click away, and there's always a new friend or a piece of gossip waiting around the digital corner. But just like any bustling reunion, it pays to navigate the halls with a bit of caution. In this chapter, we will explore the virtual hallways safely, ensuring that while reconnecting with old friends and discovering new interests, you also protect yourself from the digital equivalent of spilled punch on your party outfit. Remember, learning digital safety is not as daunting as it may seem. With the proper guidance, you can navigate the digital age with confidence. You can start small and build up your skills step by step.

Navigating Online Safety: Protecting Yourself on the Internet

Understanding Online Threats

Let's start with the basics—know what you're up against. The internet is a bit like an enormous flea market; there's a lot of treasure, some trash, and a few pickpockets, too. These pickpockets lurk in the form of phishing scams, malware, and various other digital nuisances. Phishing, for instance, involves someone trying to trick you into giving away your personal information, such as your bank account numbers or passwords. You might get an email that seems like it's from your bank, asking you to verify your account details. But here's the kicker: The bank will never ask for your sensitive information via email.

Malware, on the other hand, is malicious software that can be installed on your computer or smartphone without your consent. It can wreak havoc, from stealing your personal information to making your device as slow as snail mail. The key to avoiding these threats is vigilance. Be cautious with emails from unknown sources and think twice before clicking links or downloading attachments. Remember, if something looks out of place or too good to be true, it probably is.

Secure Internet Practices

Now, securing your digital life doesn't require being a tech whiz; think of it as more like locking your doors at night. It's about taking the necessary steps to secure your information. Start with strong passwords. Forget your pet's name followed by 123. Instead, mix it up with a combination of letters, numbers, and symbols. For example, a strong password could be "P@ssw0rd! 23" or "Tru3L0v3&Peace". Consider using a phrase or a series of unrelated words that are easy for you to remember but hard for others to guess, like "sunflower-dog-ocean." This makes your password both stronger and more secure while still being simple enough for you to recall.

Two-factor authentication (2FA) is your next layer of security. It's like having a double lock on your door. Even if someone guesses your password, they won't be able to access your account without the second form of identification, which is usually a code sent to your phone. This means that even if someone manages to crack your password, they still need your phone to get into your account. Enable this feature on all your accounts, especially those related to financial or personal information.

As for your home Wi-Fi, secure it with a strong password, and never share it with anyone you don't trust. Also, keep your network's firmware up to date to protect against vulnerabilities. Think of it as updating your house's locks to keep the burglars out.

Safe Browsing Techniques

Safe browsing is akin to knowing which neighborhoods are safe to walk through at night. Always look for HTTPS in the URL when visiting a website; the "S" stands for secure, meaning the site encrypts your data, keeping it safe from eavesdroppers. Be wary of online shopping sites that don't have HTTPS, especially if they want your credit card details.

When adjusting the privacy settings on websites and browsers, think of it as setting your boundaries in a crowded room. Customize these settings according to what you're comfortable sharing. A lot of websites and social media platforms offer privacy tutorials, and going through them can really boost your online safety. Plus, it only takes a few minutes, and you'll learn how to control what others see and share about you online.

Dealing With Suspicious Activities

If you ever bump into something suspicious online—say, a strange email, an unexpected request for money, a link that looks dubious, or a pop-up claiming your computer is infected with a virus—here's what to do: Stop. Think. Do not click. Report phishing attempts to the official email provided by your email service provider or directly to the organization being impersonated. If you accidentally download something harmful, most antivirus programs can step in to help clean things up. Plus, many of them also offer real-time protection to catch threats before they become a problem. Remember, it's better to be safe and report than to be sorry.

Safely navigating the digital age safely is about staying informed, being cautious, and using common sense. Just like you learned to cross the street, you can learn the ropes of the digital highway. With the right precautions, you can enjoy all the benefits of the digital world without any pitfalls. So, explore this digital age with confidence and a sense of adventure. There's a whole world waiting for you at your fingertips!

Video Chatting with Family: A Step-By-Step Guide

The modern marvel of video chatting! It's not just a tool; it's a gateway to a world of connections. Gone are the days of waiting for handwritten letters or costly long-distance phone calls to catch up with loved ones. Today, a grandchild's first steps, a niece's graduation, or a friend's new puppy are just a click away, thanks to video chatting platforms like Skype, Zoom, and FaceTime. These platforms don't just close the physical gap – they help you feel connected to your loved ones and share in their special moments. Many even let you create new memories together through virtual experiences. But before you dive into these digital interactions, let's sift through which platform might become your new favorite way to stay connected.

Picking the right platform is kind of like choosing the perfect hat for a sunny day, you want it to fit just right, look great, and feel comfortable. And, just like with hats, sometimes it's about finding one that's versatile enough for different situations. Skype is one of the old guards of video chatting, and it is well-suited for one-on-one conversations or small groups. It's user-friendly, which is a big tick for those who prefer straightforward tech. Zoom has risen in popularity due to its robust features that handle large groups beautifully, making it ideal for family reunions or virtual get-togethers with multiple friends. Then there's FaceTime, exclusive to Apple users, which offers a sleek interface and integrates seamlessly with other Apple devices. Think about what's most important to you: Is it the tool's simplicity, the ability to host multiple people, or the integration with your existing devices? Once you pinpoint your needs, picking the platform will be a breeze.

Setting up an account can feel like learning a new dance step, but it's smooth sailing once you get the hang of it. Let's take Skype as an example. You'll start by downloading the Skype application on your computer or smartphone. Open the app, and you'll be prompted to create an account. You can sign up using an email address or a phone number, and then you'll set up a password. Remember, a strong and unique password is the way to go! After the initial setup, you'll be asked to create a profile. Add a friendly picture of yourself and perhaps a few words to your bio. Tweaking your privacy settings is important, make sure you're okay with who can see your profile and reach out to you. And don't forget to check these settings regularly, since updates can sometimes change things without you noticing.

Making and receiving calls is the real joy of video chatting. On Skype, you can easily search for contacts by their name, email, or phone number and add them to your contact list. To start a video call:

1. Just click on the video icon next to their name. If someone's calling you, a window will pop up with their name, and you can either accept or decline the call.
2. If you encounter issues like no sound or a frozen screen, don't panic.
3. Check your internet connection first, as a weak signal is often the culprit.
4. Ensure your device's camera and microphone are enabled in the settings, and close any unnecessary applications that might be hogging your bandwidth.

Enhancing your video chat experiences can turn a simple call into a memorable event. Features like background filters can add a dash of fun or privacy to your calls.

On Zoom, you can choose a virtual background that replaces your real background with an image or video. It's perfect for those days when your house isn't as tidy as you'd like or if you want to keep your location private. Screen sharing is another fantastic tool for showing photos from your latest trip or demonstrating a recipe. Most platforms have a "share screen" button that lets you choose which part of your screen to share. If you're celebrating something special, recording the call is a great way to save those memories. Just remember to get everyone's permission before hitting record so everyone feels comfortable.

Navigating the world of video chatting can open up new avenues for staying in touch, sharing moments, and reducing the miles between us. Whether it's a weekly chat with your kids, a book club meetup, or a birthday celebration, video calls help us stay connected no matter the distance. They make it easy to keep traditions alive, even when we're miles apart. So, pick your platform, set up your account, and start connecting. The smiles of your family and friends are just a click away, ready to light up your screen and your heart.

Online Shopping Made Simple

Online shopping is the modern-day treasure hunt where the prizes are as varied as your imagination, and you don't even have to leave your comfy chair to partake! Now that you're more connected digitally, why not transform your shopping experience from traditional store hopping to clicking through cyberspace? It's like having all the stores you could ever want right at your fingertips, whether you're after the latest gadgets or unique handmade crafts from halfway around the world. And the best part? You can shop from the comfort of your own home, all while sipping your favorite drink! But before you start filling your digital cart, let's walk through the basics to ensure your online shopping spree is smooth, savvy, and secure.

Getting started with online shopping is akin to learning to ride a bicycle—once you get the hang of it, it's a breeze. First, you'll want to identify reputable online stores. You can usually count on big names like Amazon, eBay, and Walmart since they have solid systems to keep your transactions safe. Plus, they often have reliable customer service if you run into any issues along the way. However, part of the fun is discovering new niche shops that may offer something unique. When venturing into less familiar territory, a good practice is to look for trust signals on the website, such as contact information, a physical address, and a secure URL—prefixed by "https://"—which indicates that the site is protected by SSL encryption. Creating an account is typically the next step, requiring you to enter details such as your name, email, and a strong password. Remember, your email will be your username for most shopping sites, and about that password, make it a good one! Mix up letters, numbers, and symbols to create a digital key that's tough to crack.

Now, onto the nitty-gritty: ensuring your transactions are secure. This step is crucial because, let's face it, the internet can sometimes feel like the Wild West of digital data. Most trustworthy sites give you a bunch of payment options, whether you prefer using credit cards, PayPal, or even cryptocurrencies these days. It's nice to have choices that fit your preferences and make shopping a breeze. Each has its merits, but credit cards and PayPal often provide additional layers of buyer protection, including dispute resolution and fraud protection. PayPal, for instance, keeps your financial details private from sellers, adding an extra layer of security. Another tip is to use a credit card dedicated solely to online purchases. If your card details are ever compromised, the fallout won't spread to your primary financial accounts.

Comparing prices and reading reviews are equivalent to trying clothes in a fitting room. Just as you wouldn't buy a jacket without ensuring a good fit, don't rush to purchase an item online without a bit of research. Most online platforms have customer reviews and ratings, which can really help you gauge the product's quality and the seller's trustworthiness. They're a great way to see what others have experienced before making your decision. Take the time to sift through these reviews, paying attention to positive and negative feedback. For price comparisons, tools like Google Shopping or apps like ShopSavvy can help you scan across various stores to find the best deal. This can be especially handy during big sale events like Black Friday or Cyber Monday, where prices fluctuate wildly.

Lastly, tracking your orders and managing returns is like keeping tabs on your garden's growth. Once you place an order, most sites will provide a tracking number that lets you see exactly where your package is in the shipping process. It's like watching your order make its journey right to your doorstep. Keep an eye on delivery times and be aware of the return policies. Should an item not meet your expectations, or if it arrives looking nothing like its picture online, knowing how to navigate the return process can save you a lot of headaches. And it's always a good idea to reach out to customer service if you have any questions, they can often help clarify things. Most sites have a section detailing how to return items; some even offer free returns, making the process painless and straightforward.

Embracing online shopping can open up a new world of convenience and variety. It's like having a global marketplace at your command, where you can discover unique products, compare prices without walking a single step, and have your purchases delivered right to your door. You can shop at any time of day, making it super convenient for your busy schedule. With these tips, you're well-equipped to dive into the digital shopping world with confidence and savvy, making the most of your online adventures.

Using Apps to Monitor Health and Wellness

Choosing from the countless health and wellness apps can be a bit like trying to pick the healthiest cereal at the grocery store; it can feel like a lot. With so many options out there, it can be tough to figure out which ones really fit your needs. But fret not, because just like finding that perfect bowl of oats that isn't just a spoonful of sugar, picking the right health apps can significantly simplify managing your medical appointments, medication schedules, and daily fitness routines. Let's walk through how to make these apps work for you, keeping your health in check with the tap of a finger.

First, selecting the right app can feel like online dating; there are plenty of options, but finding the one that clicks with your needs is key. Start by identifying what you need most in your health management. Are you looking for something to remind you to take your medication or an app that logs your blood pressure or sugar levels? Maybe you need a comprehensive tool that does a bit of everything. Apps like MyTherapy offer medication reminders, symptom trackers, and even health reports you can share with your doctor. For fitness tracking, consider apps like Fitbit or MyFitnessPal, which can help monitor your physical activities and dietary habits. Suppose you're managing specific health conditions like diabetes. In that case, the Heartwise Blood Pressure Tracker can be handy for monitoring your cardiovascular health. The key is to pick user-friendly apps with simple interfaces that don't make you feel like you need to be a tech expert. It's also helpful to look for apps that offer tutorials or guides to get you started. Look for apps with high ratings and positive reviews in your app store, often indicating reliability and user satisfaction.

Now, let's talk about setting up these apps. Once you've downloaded your chosen health app, you'll probably be prompted to create an account. This might involve entering basic information like your name, age, and perhaps some details about your health condition. These details help personalize your experience, ensuring the app's recommendations and reminders are explicitly tailored to your needs. Many apps will walk you through their key features step-by-step when you first open them, showing you how to log your medications, schedule appointments, or input your daily meals and activities. Take your time to explore these features and customize the settings to match your daily routine. It can make a big difference in how effectively you use the app, so don't rush it; finding what works best for you is worth it. For example, if you take medication at 8 a.m. daily, set a reminder that pings you at that exact time. Or, if you prefer logging your meals right after you eat, adjust the app's mealtime settings to align with your regular dining schedule.

Privacy and data security are paramount, especially concerning your health information. It is essential to understand what data your app is collecting and how it's being used. Always read the privacy policy before diving in—yes, it can be tedious, but it's worth the peace of mind. Look for apps that use encryption to protect your data, ensuring that any health information you enter is stored securely. Be cautious about apps that require unnecessary permissions, like access to your contacts or photos, as these can be red flags for privacy concerns. It's a good idea to read reviews and do a bit of research on the app's security practices before you download. Adjust the app's privacy settings according to your comfort level, and only share the information you feel is necessary for the app's function.

Integrating these apps into your healthcare routine can amplify their benefits. Many health apps offer features that allow you to share reports with your healthcare provider, making it easier to keep them updated on your condition between visits. Discuss with your doctor which health metrics are crucial to monitor and see if they can recommend any specific apps that integrate well with their management plans. Some apps can sync directly with electronic health records, further streamlining the process. This integration helps maintain an accurate and comprehensive health log. It can also alert you to important health reminders, ensuring you never miss a check-up or medication. It also ensures that your doctor has all the necessary information to tailor your care effectively.

By using these digital tools, you're not just making health management easier; you're also taking a proactive step toward a healthier, more informed lifestyle. Having all that information at your fingertips can really motivate you to stick to your wellness goals. Whether it's keeping tabs on your heart rate, managing your medications, or tracking your daily steps, health and wellness apps can be a fantastic addition to your healthcare regimen, giving you confidence and control over your well-being. So go ahead, tap into the world of health apps, and turn your smartphone into a tool that connects you with others and a healthier future.

Exploring New Hobbies Online: Virtual Classes and Workshops

Who said learning new tricks is only for the young or the furry? In this golden era of digital exploration, the world is literally at your fingertips. It's buzzing with virtual classes and workshops that can turn any curious retiree into a budding chef, artist, or tech guru. And the best part? You can learn at your own pace, fitting it around your schedule whenever it works for you. Are you ready to dive into the ocean of online learning? Let's make a splash and discover how to start this exciting voyage from the comfort of your home.

Finding the perfect online class that aligns with your interests is like searching for the ideal seashell on a vast beach. Start by identifying what piques your interest. Have you always wanted to perfect your culinary skills or wanted to unleash your inner Picasso? Is decoding the mysteries of your smartphone what excites you? Once you've pinpointed your interest, it's time to find a class that matches your enthusiasm. Websites like Udemy, Coursera, and even YouTube are treasure troves of courses covering many subjects. Use their search functions to narrow down your choices. For instance, typing "beginner watercolor painting" or "iPhone photography tips" will yield various options. Review the course descriptions, watch intro videos if available, and, most importantly, check the reviews. Reviews can provide insight into the course's effectiveness and the instructor's teaching style, ensuring the class matches your learning preferences. They can also highlight any unique features of the course that might make it even more appealing.

Once you've hoisted your flag and are ready to sail into online learning, registering for your chosen class is your next step. This process is usually straightforward: Create an account on the platform offering the course, which typically involves providing your email and creating a password. Next, enroll in the course, which might be free or paid. Payment procedures are generally secure and user-friendly. After enrollment, you'll access all the course materials, including video lectures, reading assignments, and interactive forums. Many platforms also offer mobile apps, allowing you to access your course anytime, whether sipping coffee in your living room or relaxing in your garden. Plus, being able to learn on the go means you can fit education into even the busiest of schedules.

Participating effectively in your online class involves more than just watching videos and reading materials. Engage actively by taking notes as you would in a traditional classroom. Many courses offer discussion boards where you can ask questions and interact with fellow learners. It's a great way to share insights and get different perspectives, making the learning experience even richer. So, don't shy away from these community features. Participating in discussions can enhance your understanding of the subject and provide a sense of community and support, making the learning process informative and enjoyable.

Creating an ideal learning environment at home plays a crucial role in your online education journey. Choose a quiet, comfortable spot in your home with minimum interruptions. This could be a small desk in your bedroom or a cozy corner in your living room. Ensure your seating is comfortable and your computer or tablet is set up at a comfortable viewing height. Good lighting is crucial for reading material and reducing strain on your eyes. If you're engaging in a more interactive workshop, like a live cooking class, ensure your setup includes all the tools at arm's reach so you can easily follow along without scrambling through your kitchen drawers. Remember, the physical environment can significantly impact your learning efficiency and overall experience. Don't forget to eliminate any distractions, turn off your phone notifications, or find a quiet spot to help you stay focused.

Embracing online classes and workshops is about learning new skills and enriching your life's tapestry with vibrant threads of knowledge and interaction. Each class you take builds your abilities, confidence, and connections with others sharing your interests. So, explore with excitement, enjoy the journey, and turn your retirement into a meaningful time of growth and new experiences. Who knows what new passions you will uncover in this exciting digital landscape?

The Basics of Social Networking Sites

Welcome to the bustling world of social networking sites, where connecting with others, sharing insights, and exploring interests is all in a day's play! Think of these platforms as your digital playgrounds—places where you can meet old friends, make new ones, and stay engaged with the communities and topics you love. Let's start with a quick tour of the big players: Facebook, Twitter, and LinkedIn.

Facebook is like the town square of the digital world. It's where people come to share news, celebrate life events, and engage in discussions about everything under the sun. From photos of your grandchild's first steps to your thoughts on the latest bestseller, Facebook is a space to connect with family and friends and participate in special interest groups that match your hobbies and passions. It's really an easy way to share and discover events happening in your community.

Twitter, on the other hand, is like a bustling café. It's vibrant and fast-paced, where conversations are quick and to the point, limited to 280 characters. It's perfect for catching real-time updates, engaging with public figures, and participating in global discussions on events as they unfold. Whether following your favorite authors or joining conversations on topics you care about, Twitter keeps you at the pulse of the world's happenings.

LinkedIn is the professional wing of the social networking world. Think of it as a networking event where you can connect with professionals from various fields, join industry groups, and share your professional accomplishments. Whether you're retired or exploring new opportunities, LinkedIn is a valuable resource for staying connected with the professional community and keeping abreast of industry trends. It can also help you to connect with former colleagues or even discover mentorship opportunities

Setting up your social media profile is like setting up your stall at a fair. You want it to represent you well and attract the kind of interactions you enjoy. Start by choosing a profile picture that reflects your personality, perhaps a smiling photo from your last vacation or a casual shot from a family gathering. When filling out your profile, include information to help others understand who you are and what interests you. But remember, it's like your digital house, so lock your doors where needed. Adjust your privacy settings to control who can see your posts and personal information. Platforms like Facebook allow you to customize these settings extensively, ensuring that you share only what you feel comfortable with, keeping your digital persona safe and sound. Regularly reviewing these settings can help you stay updated on any new features or changes that could affect your privacy.

Connecting with others is the heart of social networking. Start by finding family and friends and sending them a friend request or a follow. Most platforms have a search bar where you can type a name and easily find people you know. Once connected, take the plunge and join groups or forums that spark your interest. Love gardening? There's a group for that. Do you adore mystery novels? There's a group for that, too. These spaces are fantastic for sharing ideas, asking questions, and finding community support.

Sharing content is a beautiful way to express yourself and exchange ideas. Still, it's like cooking for a potluck—you want to bring something enjoyable and appropriate. Consider who will see it when posting, whether it's a photo, a comment, or a share. Keep your posts respectful and positive, and respect others' privacy by not sharing personal conversations or photos without consent. It's also a good idea to think before you post and consider how your words might be received by others in the community. If you're unsure whether something is appropriate to share, it's best to err on the side of caution.

Navigating social networking sites can be a delightful way to enhance your digital experience, offering avenues for connection, learning, and sharing that enrich your life. As you explore these digital spaces, just remember to find a balance by respecting your own privacy and the vibe of the community. With these tools, you're set to make the most of the social networking landscape, building bridges and fostering connections that enhance your journey in the digital world.

As we wrap up our exploration of social networking sites, remember that these platforms are tools for enhancing your connections and enriching your life with new interactions and learning opportunities. They are gateways to maintain relationships, discover interests, and engage with communities that share your passions. As you confidently navigate the digital age, these social platforms can become integral to your vibrant online presence, bringing joy and valuable connections into your daily life. The endings are just beginnings, and the golden age is a new start. So, get out there and start living the beginning of the rest of your life to the fullest. Remember, every day is an opportunity to try something new and make wonderful memories.

Conclusion

Well, here we are at the end of our little adventure together. Reflecting back, we've traveled quite a distance, haven't we? From those initial uncertain steps—viewing retirement as just a long stretch of Sundays—to seeing it as a canvas colored with endless possibilities. It's not the final curtain; it's the grand opening to a second act filled with vibrancy and the thrill of discovery. It's actually a chance to reconnect with old passions or explore new interests you never had time for before

Throughout our chapters, we've tackled everything from the magic of smartphones to the gentle rhythms of Tai Chi, from the creative escapes of painting and poetry to the simple joys of a well-tended garden. We've welcomed technology, not as something confusing or scary but as a friend that helps us stay connected with the people we care about and the world outside our windows. We've discussed the importance of knitting together strong social fibers and maintaining those old bridges while daring to build new ones.

Key to our journey has been the wellness theme—both the body and the mind. Remember, stretching isn't just for yoga mats, and mental exercises aren't confined to crossword puzzles on Sunday paper. They're part of a broader commitment to keeping ourselves spry and spirited, ready to leap (or step cautiously) into whatever each new day holds.

And speaking of days ahead, don't let this be the end of your quest. Retirement is not a static state but a phase of continuous exploration and growth. There's a world of new skills and hobbies out there just waiting to spark your curiosity. Why not pick up that guitar gathering dust in the corner or dive into the history of that place you've always wanted to visit? Every day is a fresh page to start something new. Plus, connecting with others who share your interests can make the journey even more enjoyable.

So, what's your next step? Pick one thing we've discussed that sparks a light in your eyes, whether it's joining a walking club, starting a blog, or maybe just setting a time each day to meditate. Dive into it with the enthusiasm of a kid at the start of summer vacation.

It's perfectly normal to feel a bit adrift as you adjust to this new rhythm of life. Remember, this book isn't just a read; it's a companion for this journey. Use it to remind yourself that with the freedom of retirement comes an incredible opportunity to redefine yourself, explore, learn, and grow in ways you never imagined. Take this time to discover new passions and maybe even meet new friends along the way.

I encourage you not to keep your stories and successes to yourself. Could you share them? Whether over coffee, on a Facebook post, or a call to an old friend, your stories can light the way for others, just as they illuminate your own path.

As we part ways in this final chapter, I leave you with this thought: *Retirement is not the end of the road but the beginning of the open highway.* May your journey be filled with health, laughter, and discovery. Approach each day with optimism and a heart open to new adventures. After all, the best part of the journey is the surprise and enjoyment along the way. And don't forget to celebrate your small victories; they make the adventure even more rewarding

Here's to your next adventure—may it be one for the books!

References

The Benefits of Low-Impact Exercise For Seniors. (n.d.). Spectrum CommunityServices.https://www.spectrumcs.org/about/blog/333-the-benefits-of-low-impact-exercise-for-seniors

The Best Budgeting Apps for Seniors. (n.d.). Senior Living. https://www.seniorliving.org/finance/budgeting-apps/

Best Social Media Apps for Seniors and How to Use Them Safely. (n.d.). Senior Helpers. https://www.seniorhelpers.com/fl/south-palm-beach/resources/blogs/best-social-media-apps-for-seniors-and-how-to-use-them-safely/

Birding For Beginners. (n.d.). U.S. National Park Service. https://www.nps.gov/articles/birding-for-beginners.htm

The Cognitive Benefits of Lifelong Learning for Seniors. (n.d.). Knute Nelson. https://www.knutenelson.org/news-stories/lifelong-learning-benefits

The Complete Guide to Writing a Memoir. (n.d.). Palmetto Publishing. https://www.palmettopublishing.com/resources/the-complete-guide-to-writing-a-memoir

Creativity and art therapies to promote healthy aging. (2022). National Center for Biotechnology Information. https://www.ncbi.nlm.nih.gov/pmc/articles/PMC9549330/

8 Great Travel Apps for Seniors. (n.d.). Torrance Memorial. https://www.torrancememorial.org/healthy-living/blog/8-great-travel-apps-for-seniors/

18 Free or Cheap Activities for Seniors. (n.d.). The Penny Hoarder. https://www.thepennyhoarder.com/save-money/free-or-cheap-activities-for-seniors/

Empower Seniors with Cooking Classes. (n.d.). Butterball Food Service. https://www.butterballfoodservice.com/resources/empower-seniors-with-cooking-classes/

FaceTime for Seniors: An Easy Step-by-Step Guide. (n.d.). Senior Living. https://www.seniorliving.org/cell-phone/facetime-for-seniors/

Five Ways Mindfulness Helps You Age Better. (2021). Greater Good Science Center at UC Berkeley. https://greatergood.berkeley.edu/article/item/five_ways_mindfulness_helps_you_age_better

Free Community Programs. (n.d.). Clayworks. https://www.clayworksinc.org/communityprograms

Fueling multigenerational connection through game nights. (n.d.). United Healthcare. https://www.uhc.com/news-articles/newsroom/game-night

A Good Night's Sleep. (n.d.). National Institute on Aging. https://www.nia.nih.gov/health/sleep/good-nights-sleep

How to get started with chair yoga. (n.d.). University of Arkansas System Division of Agriculture.

https://www.uaex.uada.edu/life-skills-wellness/health/physical-activity-resources/chair-yoga.aspx

How to start a seniors' social club. (n.d.). Town Lively. https://townlively.com/how-to-start-a-seniors-social-club/

How To Start Book Clubs for Seniors: Your Guide. (n.d.). Book Riot. https://bookriot.com/book-clubs-for-seniors/
9 Musical Instruments That Seniors Can Easily Learn. (n.d.). Seniority. https://seniority.in/blog/9-musical-instruments-that-seniors-can-easily-learn

Online Learning for Seniors: 6 Of The Best Free... (n.d.). StoryPoint. https://www.storypoint.com/resources/health-wellness/online-learning-for-seniors/

Retirement and Beyond: Exploring Volunteer Opportunities for Seniors. (n.d.). Senior Site. https://seniorsite.org/resource/retirement-and-beyond-exploring-volunteer-opportunities-for-seniors/

Retirement Hobbies for Better Mental Health. (n.d.). SunLife. https://www.sunlife.co.uk/articles-guides/your-life/retirement-hobbies-for-better-mental-health/

The Senior's Guide to Online Safety. (n.d.). Connect Safely. https://connectsafely.org/seniors-guide-to-online-safety/

7 Essential Benefits of Water Aerobics for Seniors. (n.d.). Spring Hills. https://www.springhills.com/resources/water-aerobics-for-seniors

Start a Walking Group - Create the Good. (n.d.). AARP. https://createthegood.aarp.org/volunteer-guides/start-walking-group.html

Starting a Business in Retirement: Retiree Business Ideas. (n.d.). ZenBusiness. https://www.zenbusiness.com/starting-business-retirement/

Travel Discounts for Seniors. (n.d.). U.S. News & World Report. https://money.usnews.com/money/retirement/aging/articles/travel-discounts-for-seniors

24 Colleges With Free Tuition for Senior Citizens. (n.d.). Best Colleges. https://www.bestcolleges.com/blog/free-college-tuition-senior-citizens/

USDA MyPlate Nutrition Information for Older Adults. (n.d.). MyPlate. https://www.myplate.gov/life-stages/older-adults

Volunteer Work Can Improve Your Physical And Mental Health In Retirement. (2023). Forbes. https://www.forbes.com/sites/nextavenue/2023/12/30/volunteer-work-can-improve-your-physical-and-mental-health-in-retirement/

Volunteering and Subsequent Health and Well-being in Older Adults: An Outcome-Wide Longitudinal Approach. (2020). National Center for Biotechnology Information. https://www.ncbi.nlm.nih.gov/pmc/articles/PMC7375895/

End of Book Review

Title: Embracing Fun in Retirement

Subtitle: Boost Wellness, Build Social Connections, and Explore Affordable Adventures

Well, Here We Are!

We've traveled quite a distance together, haven't we? From those first unsure steps, thinking retirement was just a long stretch of Sundays, to seeing it as a colorful canvas full of endless possibilities. Retirement isn't the final curtain—it's the grand opening to a new, exciting chapter filled with discovery and joy.

In **"Embracing Fun in Retirement"** by **Danny Toam**, we've explored many fun and exciting things. From learning the magic of smartphones to the calming practice of Tai Chi, from the creativity of painting and writing poetry to the simple joys of gardening, we've seen how retirement can be an adventure. Technology has become our friend, connecting us with loved ones and the world outside our windows. We've also discussed the importance of keeping our minds and bodies healthy with stretching, mental exercises, and more.

What's Next?

Retirement is not a time to stop—it's a time to keep growing and exploring. There are so many new skills and hobbies waiting to be discovered. The joy of picking up that dusty guitar or learning about the history of a place you've always wanted to visit can be truly exhilarating. Every day is a new page in your adventure story, filled with excitement and new experiences.

Share Your Adventure!

Your stories and experiences are not just important; they are invaluable. They can inspire others and light the way for fellow adventurers. Whether over coffee, in a Facebook post, or over the phone with an old friend, sharing your journey helps everyone find joy and excitement in retirement. Your experiences are what make this community vibrant and supportive.

How to Share Your Review

1. **Think Back:** What was your favorite part of the book? Did something make you smile or excited to try something new?

2. **Rate the Fun:** How fun has the book been for you so far? Give it a score!

3. **Share Your Adventures:** Have you tried any of the activities? How did it go?

4. **Look Forward:** What are you most excited about in the rest of the book?

Ready to Share?

Click Here to Submit Your Review!

https://www.amazon.com/review/review-your-purchases/?asin=BOOKASIN

Enjoy the rest of your adventure with "Embracing Fun in Retirement"! We can't wait to hear all about it.

Here's to your next adventure—may it be one for the books!

www.ingramcontent.com/pod-product-compliance
Lightning Source LLC
Chambersburg PA
CBHW051214120626
46547CB00013B/1350